SOUND
FOR
THE
THEAT

DEDICATION

People enter the theatre for many reasons. In my case I was fortunate, as a small boy, to enjoy the encouragement, professionalism and enthusiasm of the late Jack Mathews, and of the legendary Bill Platt, stage director and chief electrician respectively of the London Palladium, which itself played no small part in my seduction. This book is dedicated to that magical theatre, and to the men who made it so.

SOUND FOR THE THEATRE

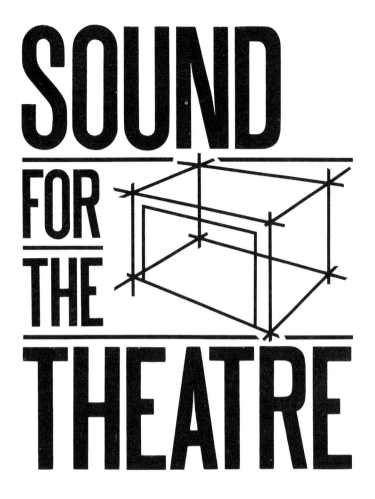

Graham Walne

A & C Black · London
Theatre Arts Books/Routledge · New York

First published in this form 1990
A & C Black (Publishers) Ltd
35 Bedford Row, London WC1R 4JH

ISBN 0–7136–3135–X

Based on Sound for Theatres, one of the City Arts
Series, first published 1981 by John Offord
(Publications) Ltd.

© 1990 and 1981 Graham Walne

A CIP catalogue record for this book is
available from the British Library.

Published simultaneously in U.S.A. by
Theatre Art Books/Routledge
29 West 35 Street, New York, NY 10001

ISBN 087830–119–4

Library Congress data available.

Printed in Great Britain
by Whitstable Litho Ltd,
Whitstable, Kent

CONTENTS

SECTION ONE – SOUND THEORY

SECTION TWO – ACOUSTICS

SECTION THREE – EQUIPMENT

SECTION FOUR – SYSTEM DESIGN

SECTION FIVE – COMMUNICATION AND EFFECTS SYSTEMS

SECTION SIX – APPENDICES

PREFACE

In the preface to **Sound for Theatres** published in 1981, I stated that the purpose of the book was to 'assist managers, students, technicians, and performers in their work...to explain the terminology and technology of theatre sound in a single volume...to provide a comprehensive work of basic reference and...to keep the language simple without shirking from explaining some of the most complex problems that can be encountered.' I would like to think that this book remains true to that purpose.

The sound landscape has altered considerably in the nine years since the above words were written, therefore much of this book is new. Budgets are more realistic today; the sound system which I specified recently for Reading Hexagon cost £100,000, even allowing for inflation a sum of that magnitude would have been unthinkable in 1981 for a regional theatre, today it represents the respect for the medium and the professionalism of the Hexagon's management. Overall the marriage between equipment and acoustics has been cemented in the last nine years. In 1981 many acoustic calculations were known but were not as widely used as they are today, typical is the system for calculating articulation losses which is now included in this book. This kind of respect for the science, and the greater availability of resources has produced new design solutions such as the centre loudspeaker cluster, now explained in these pages. And of course the digital revolution now touches everybody and every system in some way and promises to transform the landscape over the lifetime of this edition, hence this book contains an introduction to digital audio.

It remains for me to thank John Offord for the genesis of this book, Anna Bargus and Karen Kenwick for all their hours at my word processor and Barry Evans for his illustrations. I should also like to thank all at A & C Black, firstly for their interest, and then for their patience.

Graham Walne

INTRODUCTION

A sound system is a chain and so this book is about that chain.

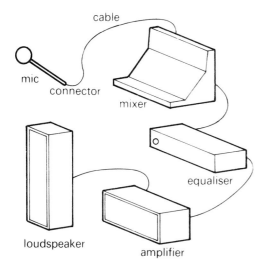

The sound chain

The chain begins with acoustics because any sound system must be married to the auditorium it serves and so the effects of room shapes, building and furnishing materials must be appreciated. The vital links of microphone, mixer, amplifier and loudspeaker come next and here it is vital that there are no compromises otherwise the overall sound will only be as good as the weakest link, often this is the electrical installation. All of these subjects are explained here.

Sound system design today is a complex subject and the manager will almost certainly be obliged to rely on outside advice when thinking of a new system, he would be wise to think of a consultant. Internal staff frequently lack broad experience and suppliers cannot be expected to offer advice free of commercial interest. This process is also 'shadowed by the rigours of the lowest tender system and unless the specification is accurate, councils and boards will make the wrong choice. Little wonder that many systems are poor and that most companies and performers tour their own system.

This book aims to help understand the chain, but two rather vital links in the chain are missing.

The mouth is of course the starting point in our chain but the one over which we have the least control; more and more performers today cannot project and place too much reliance on the sound system; in these circumstances we must recognise that any sound system, however good, cannot work miracles. At the end of the chain is the ear, and since each member of the audience is different each will perceive the sound differently (hopefully this book will help the manager to deal with complaints!).

The first section explains the basics of sound and the language we shall meet.

SECTION ONE – SOUND THEORY

ORIGINS

All sounds are produced by causing a membrane to vibrate. For example when the strings of a guitar are plucked, or our vocal chords excited by air being exhaled from the lungs, the air particles adjacent to the vibrating chords or strings are pushed out of position and they pass the effect of this collision from one particle to the next, just as a line of dominoes does when the first one is pushed over. This energy is transmitted all the way to our ear drum where the vibrations are turned into tiny electrical impulses and passed to our brain.

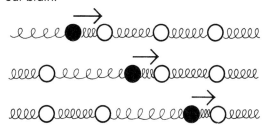

THE VIBRATION OF THE AIR
Each particle can move slightly out of position and when it does so it knocks into the next particle passing the effect of the vibration down the line before returning to rest.

Another analogy often used to illustrate how sound behaves is that of the effect of a stone being dropped into a pond. The ripples on the pond spread out in all directions and, like sound waves, they decrease in strength the further they travel away from the source of the disturbance. The wave on the pond also forms exactly the shape of the wave of a vibration, it starts from a position of rest, is vibrated to a peak of activity, back through its original position to a trough and then to a position of rest.

The distance from the crest of one sound wave to the crest of the next is called the wavelength (although we could measure this from any point on one wave to the same point on the next) and the two identical points are said to be in phase. The length of the soundwaves (wavelengths) that we can hear ranges from one inch to forty feet (2.5cm to 12.25 metres) and in acoustics we need to relate the behaviour of a sound in a room to the dimensions of the room. This is because if a sound has a wavelength identical to or multiple of the dimension between two surfaces in the room (usually parallel side walls) then this sound can be unduly emphasised. This is called a standing wave and we shall see later that because these can be either useful or harmful we need to be able to control them.

However we rarely talk of wavelengths in sound system design. Our identification of sounds is done by counting the number of times the source makes complete vibrations in one second. These used to be termed cycles per second – cps, but are now named after the 19th Century engineer, Hertz, abbreviated to Hz (and kHz in the case of quantities of 1000). Sounds which vibrate many times each second are known as high frequency – HF (commonly known as treble) and those which vibrate rather fewer times each second are called low frequency – LF (commonly known as bass).

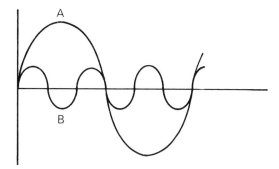

FREQUENCY
Sine wave of two vibrations, from rest, out in one direction then in the other and back through the position of rest. Wave A has a frequency one third of that of wave B, wave A is therefore low frequency and wave B high frequency.

DIRECTION

The pond analogy used above is slightly misleading because, unlike water ripples only low frequency sound waves spread out evenly in all directions, the higher frequency sound waves are more directional. A more useful analogy here is that of the high frequency car horn which is concerned only with providing a warning in one direction alone, whereas a low frequency ship fog horn is more concerned with warning in all directions.

This difference in the way in which low fre-

DIRECTION
Sound source A is unidirectional and can be best heard only in front (e.g. a car horn) whereas sound source B is omnidirectional and can be clearly heard on all sides (e.g. a ship's fog horn).

quency and high frequency sounds radiate is a major factor in the placing of microphones and loudspeakers. For example the omni-directional low frequency sounds will easily find their way into the microphone but the microphone must be pointed at the uni-directional high frequency sources for the best pick-up. Similarly low frequency sounds will radiate in all directions from a loudspeaker but for the best high frequency response the loudspeaker needs to be aimed at the listener. The ability of low frequency sounds to radiate indiscriminately, and hence into open microphones, is one of the causes of howlround, more commonly called feedback, and we will look at ways of reducing this later.

When placing loudspeakers sound engineers also have to take into account the ear's ability to identify the location of sound sources. The ear has difficulty in placing the location of low frequency (long wavelength) sounds, but is quite accurate in placing the location of high frequency (short wavelength) sounds. This is because high frequencies have wavelengths shorter than the distance between the ears, sounds above 1000Hz cannot reach both ears at the same time and at the same intensity, one ear is therefore favoured and this provides the clue to the direction of the source in the horizontal plane. However the ear is far less successful in locating sources of sound in the vertical plane (unless it is provided with some visual clue, when the brain computes the result). This is essentially why the common positions for loudspeakers are either at the sides of the stage – when the location of the sound is important as with effects, or over the centre of the proscenium arch – when sources need to be less evident as with vocal reinforcement.

AMPLITUDE

We have said that sound is transmitted by the vibration of air particles from a position of rest to a peak back through the position of rest to an extreme opposite. Amplitude is the distance between the extremes of the vibration and the bigger the distance the bigger the amplitude which in turn means that more energy is involved and this energy will produce more sound. Amplitude is often therefore associated with loudness, 'loudness' is in fact a specific technical term which can be measured (in sones) but since it is rarely used in sound system design, the term loudness is used here in a subjective sense.

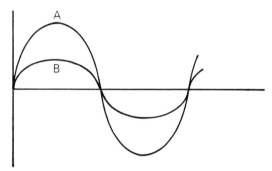

AMPLITUDE
Two sine waves of the same frequency but showing that wave A has a higher amplitude than wave B and would therefore have more strength and be the louder.

THE SPEED OF SOUND

Since sound is dependent upon vibration, it can travel through anything except a vacuum. It travels through some materials faster than others, by comparison with its speed through air sound travels about four times faster in water, about fourteen times faster in iron, whilst through rubber it slows down to about one-tenth of the air speed.

Compared to other sources, such as light which travels at 186,000 miles per second, the speed of sound is very slow. It is important to note that the speed is directly related to the temperature at the time. It is virtually constant at all frequencies, although sound does travel faster in humid air than in dry air. Humid air also absorbs more HF than LF content and so in extremely humid conditions the sound engineer would need to boost the HF part of the sound signal to compensate. As the speed of sound rises with temperature, so do the higher frequencies of many wind instruments which cannot be tuned to overcome this problem in the same way as string instruments can.

The temperature should always be taken into account in calculations where distance is involved. At 14°C the speed is 1115′ (340m) per second and this rises or falls 2ft (0.61m) per second for each degree centigrade change. There is a direct relationship between the three terms discussed in previous pages, which may be expressed thus:

$$speed\ of\ sound = \frac{wavelength}{\times\ frequency}$$

In a large auditorium, where several groups of loudspeakers might be employed, it is possible for sound to travel so slowly over the distances that amplified sounds reach some of the audience before the live sound causing a disturbing blurring of the words and confusing the listener as to the direction of the source. Electronic delays inserted in the loudspeaker system are used to overcome this and we shall look at this more closely later.

FUNDAMENTALS AND HARMONICS

The initial vibration of a sound source is known as the fundamental, and therefore the frequency produced is known as the fundamental frequency, the subsequent vibrations, which are exact multiples of the fundamental frequency, are called the harmonics. Thus a note on a musical instrument which has a fundamental of

100Hz will have a second harmonic of 200Hz, a 3rd of 300Hz and so on.

On the musical scale, the pitch of a note is the frequency by which it can be identified as a point of reference. For example by international agreement 'concert-pitch' indicates that an instrument has been tuned relative to 440Hz (although there are regional and organisational variations which employ other frequencies).

The term octave is used to denote the distance between any two frequencies which differ by a ratio of 2:1. Thus an octave separates the fundamental or first harmonic from the second harmonic, 100Hz:200Hz. At the upper end of the scale the same ratio still applies even though actual frequency numbers are larger. Thus an octave still separates the frequencies 1000Hz and 2000Hz, 10kHz and 20kHz. Two notes separated by an octave are said to be in tune. The piano keyboard is a useful place to learn about octaves since each set of eight keys spans an octave, bottom A is set at 28Hz, A above bottom A is set at 55Hz, and so on, at 110Hz, 220Hz, 440Hz, 880Hz, 1760Hz, 3520Hz, and top A at 7040Hz.

The term octave occurs again in sound system design when the output of the whole system is tuned to the acoustic of the room in order to improve quality and system gain. The device which is used is called an equaliser and it contains a number of filter controls which can boost or cut part of the sound signal. Simple equalisers are set at octave centres but since this still leaves large gaps between filters in the mid and upper frequency ranges, the most suitable equalisers have filters at one-third octave intervals to provide more control.

Whether the harmonics diminish in intensity (which is usual) or retain much of the energy depends on how the source is initially vibrated

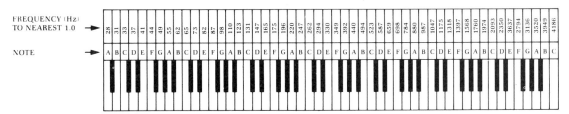

The relationship between frequency and the piano keyboard's range.

and subsequently damped and it is the strength and quantity of the harmonics which distinguishes the quality or timbre of musical instruments and makes it possible for us to identify two different instruments playing the same note. For example some wind instruments like the flute, have few harmonics and emit fairly pure tones whereas others, like the piano, have complex sounds created by a large number of harmonics.

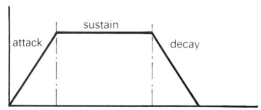

TRANSIENT RESPONSE
The way in which a sound behaves when vibrated, the slopes can vary and the sustain can be longer or shorter.

The transient response of an instrument is the way in which it behaves when its sound source is first vibrated. The start of the first vibration is called the attack, the duration is called the sustain, and the final part of the vibration is called the decay. String instruments tend to produce notes which decay, whereas wind instruments tend to sustain notes. Some instruments, especially those used in rock music have a sharp attack and it is important that the sound system can cope with the virtually instantaneous high sound levels often produced.

It may be noted from the above data that any sound system which is concerned with reproducing music to high quality requires a wide frequency response to encompass both the fundamentals and the harmonics. By contrast a speech-only system could operate satisfactorily from within a reduced width of frequency response because the human voice does not produce a wide range of fundamentals and harmonics.

THE DECIBEL – dB

In the whole sphere of sound the decibel is probably the most difficult term to understand, there are three basic points to appreciate.

Firstly, the decibel is not a unit of measurement on its own but it is a unit of comparison between two other units of measurement – the decibel can be used to compare two voltages, or two currents or two sound pressure levels (known as SPL), generally we will use the term in this latter respect to measure the sound level in the auditorium or the output of loudspeakers. Since sound pressure varies with distance, any SPL figure which does not indicate the distance from the source at which it was measured is meaningless, and as we shall see later loudspeaker measurements should also state the input power used at the time.

(The sone is another unit of measurement of loudness, and there is also the phon. These take into account the fact that the ear does not respond evenly to all frequencies. We will not be concerned with these terms in our work but they are mentioned here merely to indicate their position in the overall picture).

The second point is that whilst two other measurement figures are always involved it is common to find the decibel figure appearing on its own. Generally, but not exclusively, when this happens it means that the other figure was an agreed international reference point. Hence the decibel shows the difference between the other measurement and the international reference point. In all cases the reference point is known as zero level, or 0dB. We will meet this term mostly with respect to sound pressure level and in this respect the zero level of sound pressure is defined as the smallest sound which the ear will detect at a frequency of 1000Hz (although we should be aware that the ear is more sensitive at other frequencies).

The third point about the decibel is that it works to a logarithmic scale (exactly as our ear does) rather than to a linear scale. In other words, each time the ear detects a doubling of sound, the intensity has actually gone up by a factor of ten, i.e. ten times the original level for the first doubling, one hundred times for the second, one thousand for the third, and so on.

Now let us examine the way in which values are expressed in decibels, with respect to ratios of sound intensity and sound pressure. Sound intensity is the input energy to a device and each time it is doubled the value is increased by 3dB. A ratio of intensity that was 100:1 could be written as 10^2:1. Ignoring the :1, we would take the square factor and multiply by ten to express this ratio in decibels, 20dB. Thus a ratio of intensity of 1000:1 would be 10^3:1 or 30dB and so on.

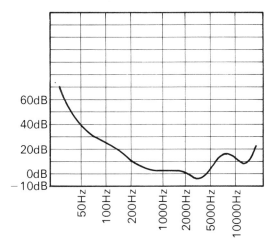

THE EAR'S SENSITIVITY
The line shows how sensitive the ear is to different frequencies, it is the most sensitive in the 2kHz to 5kHz region and if we wanted a 50hz tone to sound as loud as say a 1kHz tone then we would have to amplify if by 40dB – the difference between the two points on the left side of the graph.

Sound pressure is effectively the output – what we hear. Each time the pressure is doubled the value is increased by 6dB. For sound pressure the same exercise above still applies but the multiplying factor is 20. Thus 100:1 becomes 10^2:1, becomes $2 \times 20 = 40 = 40$dB, 1000:1 becomes 10^3:1, becomes $3 \times 20 = 60 = 60$dB.

It is also necessary to have a standard reference point for the electrical power flowing through sound equipment, so that it may be matched and appreciated when more or less power is being used. The standard is 0.001 watt. This may also be expressed as 0.775 volt across 600 ohm or as 0dBm, where the little m represents the milliwatt indicated above in the figure 0.001. The output of microphones is calibrated in this way as we shall see later for example figures quoted as above the reference value are expressed as positive: +20dB etc, and figures quoted as below that value are expressed as negative: −20dB.

THE ENDS OF THE CHAIN

Now we have dealt with the way that sound is generated and we have reviewed the vocabulary of terms we shall meet throughout the book let us turn to two elements closest to us and vital parts of the sound chain – the voice and the ear.

THE HUMAN VOICE

Human beings generate sounds by means of their vocal chords which intercept air exhaled from the lungs and vibrate to produce a note. The sound must then pass through the pharynx, the mouth and the nose and it is the way in which these cavities are used to shape the harmonics that determines the tone of the sound we hear and enables us to differentiate one voice from another.

In the case of performers it is important that they understand these facts and the necessity of voice training. Adequate breath control helps sustain the ends of words, where the vital consonants are often situated. If these are lost then clarity suffers. Singers' voices often strain to produce adequate loudness at the extreme high and low frequencies, gutteral or strident sounds result. Sadly today fewer and fewer performers are capable of clear and strong voice projection, perhaps as a result of time spent in film and television work. As a consequence more and more reliability is placed on amplifying stage productions (even those including classically trained actors). In musicals where amplification is expected the sound system cannot do all the work, the performer must understand correct microphone technique – too little voice and the microphone is likely to pick up unwanted sounds or generate feed-back in its straining to catch any level; distortion produced by working too loudly into the microphone can only be contained by expensive equipment.

When selecting loudspeakers and operating tone controls (equalisation) it is important to understand the range of frequencies produced by the human voice. The usual fundamental frequency for males is about 125Hz, and about 210Hz for females. This would be a normal voice level, but the trained voices such as those of actors and actresses have higher values of about 140Hz and 230Hz respectively.

The frequency range of trained voices is unsurprisingly wider than that of untrained voices and males usually have a wider range than females – although female voices are purer, having fewer harmonics (one reason why they tend to make better public address announcers than men). The pitch of the voice is usually raised in emotional moments and when working in chorus. Here are the frequency ranges of the various parts of our speech:

Table 1

fundamentals	125–250Hz
vowels	350–2000Hz
consonants	1500–4000Hz

Thus the response of a speech-only sound system can be concentrated within the 350–4000Hz band, but a wider band would create more realism, say one of 60–6000Hz. We shall see later that in the case of sound reinforcement systems, it is occasionally desirable to be able to raise the lower frequency limit to reduce howl-round (feedback) which often (though not exclusively) occurs when the omni-directional lower frequencies find their way too easily back into the microphone. (There are also other ways to reduce feedback as we shall see later).

Here are the frequency ranges of the fundamentals of singers:

Table 2

bass	85–340Hz
baritone	90–380Hz
tenor	125–460Hz
alto	130–680Hz
contralto	180–600Hz
soprano	225–1100Hz

It is interesting that in the frequency range 62.5–500Hz is found 60% of the human voice's power but only 5% of the intelligibility; in the 500–1000Hz range there is 35% of the power and 35% of the intelligibility but in the 1000–8000Hz range only 5% of the power but 60% of the intelligibility. We shall see later that the tone controls on many simple sound mixers lie outside this last range, generally the 'bass' is set at

60–100Hz and the 'treble' at 10kHz and therefore the mixer cannot directly affect the quality of the voice. This is why it is so important to select a mixer with more comprehensive tone controls in the middle range.

Now let us look at the sound pressure level that the human voice can produce. These are the values measured at a distance of 10' (3m).

Table 3

whisper	30dBA
conversation	50dBA
lecturer	60dBA
actor	70dBA

We have mentioned that the ear is not equally sensitive to all frequencies. A sound pressure level meter which hears in the same way we do is said to be following an 'A' weighting, hence the above measurements are made on such a meter, and as we have also seen the distance at which the measurements have been made is stated.

130 dB	
	threshold of pain
120 dB	
	loud rock music
110 dB	
	underground train
100 dB	heavy lorry
	loud classical music
90 dB	heavy street traffic
80 dB	average factory
70 dB	noisy office
	actor
60 dB	lecturer
	average office
50 dB	street
	conversation
40 dB	soft music
30 dB	quiet theatre
	whisper
20 dB	sound studio
10 dB	rustling leaves
	anechoic room
0 dB	threshold of hearing at 1kHz

SOUND PRESSURE LEVELS
Table showing how some common sounds compare with zero level

The reason that this is important is because with a point-source of sound (such as the human voice, a single musical instrument, or one type of loudspeaker design we shall meet) the

SPL dies away by 6dB every time the distance from the source is doubled (this is known as the inverse square law). Thus if a trained actor is producing 70dB at 10' this becomes 64dB at 20', 58dB at 40' and 52dB at 80' and so on. An untrained actor might produce at least 15dB less than this so that on the back row of a typical theatre, 40' from the stage, the untrained actor will produce say 43dB.

Although this is less than the level of ordinary conversation, before we can categorically say that this is insufficient without amplification we also need to know the level of the ambient sound in the auditorium, this is the level of the background noise made up of air conditioning, traffic and of the audience itself, too high an ambient level and it will mask main sound. In practical terms it is expensive to silence air-handling plant and traffic, and consequently most multipurpose establishments have ambient noise levels in the order of 30–40dBA. The optimum level has been calculated, and forms part of a national series of suggestions (called Noise Criteria or NC) for different types of buildings and uses. The level suggested relates to specific frequency bands, but the average levels for concert halls, theatres, lecture and conference halls is 20–30dBA.

It is known that in order to avoid masking there must be at least 10dB separation between the ambient noise level and the sound pressure level produced by either the actor or the sound system; many sound designers (the author included) aim for a higher figure of 25dB.

Hence if we return to our untrained actor producing 43dB on the back row and we place him in a multipurpose hall with an ambient level of 30dB then we are not only below conversational listening level but also within the danger zone for masking from the ambient sound. Hence it would be sensible to provide a sound reinforcement system in this case. Now we can use the figures in reverse. For example, we need at least 25dB separation between the ambient and the sound system. If the ambient level is 30dB then the sound pressure level produced by the system on the back row 40' from the stage must be at least 55dB; and using the 6dB rule we can therefore project that 20' from the stage the SPL must be 61dB, 10' it must be 67dB, 5' it must be 73dB. This figure then becomes the criteria for what

we need out of any sound system installed to reinforce the actor's voice.

In fact these figures should only be used as a guide, since the 6dB rule takes no account of the sound which does not die away but continues to bounce or reverberate around the theatre. This adds to the ambient SPL, so that the actual masking level is even higher. It is possible to calculate at which distance the reverberent level begins to add to that of the direct level, and this might indicate that amplification is needed since, in extreme cases, the reverberant level would hinder intelligibility. Nevertheless the 6dB rule is a good rule-of-thumb for most auditoria and later we will look at the above problem more scientifically since there it comprises a number of variable factors, the number of loudspeakers used, their performance, (since some designs do not follow the inverse square law as we will see later) and finally we need to take into account the influence of the room itself. We will also look later at an equation which enables the amount of articulation in the sound system to be calculated from these variables.

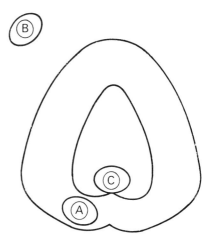

VOICE CONTOUR
An exaggerated drawing but indicating that although A is behind the actor C he will hear better than B who is outside the contour.

It has been found that a contour can be drawn for the human voice, which like most instruments is more directional at some frequencies than others. In the case of performances, actors relate to each other – and so the voice contour may be used to shape the optimum area of hearing in an auditorium. It can be seen from the above example that for an acceptable speech level the distance from the performer to the perimeter of the contour must vary with the level produced by the performer. Nevertheless – if we ignore quality for a moment – people behind the actor but within the contour will hear better than those in front but outside the contour. However since the clarity is contained in the directional upper frequencies much of the intelligibility is lost on those behind, a vital point to remember when placing people on platforms at meetings and this is where the sound reinforcement system, and the correct acoustic design of the auditorium, can help.

THE HUMAN EAR

Sound enters the ear and travels down the auditory canal to the ear drum, which vibrates. These sensations are passed to the hearing nerves by other mechanisms in the inner ear. It is the size of the auditory canal that determines how sensitive the ear is to various frequencies.

Most young people can detect, under ideal conditions, pure tones of 16–20,000Hz and this range diminishes with age, especially at the upper end. The ear is more sensitive in the range 1000–6000Hz and the most sensitive in the range 3kHz to 5kHz, achieving a level of −4dB. Should we require a sound either above or below 1000Hz or above 6000Hz to sound as loud as a frequency within that band, we should have to amplify it more.

The ear can detect a very wide range of sound pressure levels. We know that at the reference frequency of 1000Hz the quietest level the ear can detect is set as 0dB but the loudest sound, without actually incurring permanent damage, is about a million times greater at 120dB. Under ideal conditions the minimum change in intensity which an experienced ear can detect is about 1dB, in normal circumstances it is usual to assume a detection of 2 or 3dB.

HIGH SOUND LEVELS AND DEAFNESS

It is certain that prolonged exposure to a high

sound level of industrial noise produces a temporary loss of hearing and that constant exposure will lead to permanent damage. The damage is done to the nerves of the inner ear and on occasions, to the auditory nerve, initially the effect is on the higher frequencies but extends in severe cases over the whole spectrum. Until recently, hearing damage was irreversible by surgery but now electrodes can be implanted in the inner ear and connected to a small microphone placed by the ear; deaf people so equipped can now hear perfectly through this technique.

Industry is obliged to adhere to maximum levels of exposure to noise as per the following tables, it should be noted that they are measured in slightly different ways. The U.K. 'A' scale corresponds to the response of the human ear – the U.S.A. 'OSHA' scale is more concerned with linear exposure to continuous sound levels:

Table 4

U.K.

under 90dBA	no limit
90dBA	8 hours per day maximum
93dBA	4 hours per day maximum
96dBA	2 hours per day maximum
99dBA	1 hour per day maximum
102dBA	$\frac{1}{2}$ hour per day maximum
105dBA	$\frac{1}{4}$ hour per day maximum

U.S.A (OSHA) (1970)

90dBA	8 hours per day maximum
95dBA	4 hours per day maximum
100dBA	2 hours per day maximum
105dBA	1 hour per day maximum
110dBA	$\frac{1}{2}$ hour per day maximum
115dBA	$\frac{1}{4}$ hour per day maximum
over 115dBA	none

Unfortunately the above criteria cannot automatically be applied to music because it is not classified as a continuous noise – the definition is that the sound level should not fluctuate by more than 8dBA, and music usually does.

Some research into high sound pressure levels of music has been carried out on both sides of the Atlantic and the results are contradictory. Early work in Leeds suggested that frequent attendance to discos would result in some hearing loss later in life (and an attempt was made to restrict systems to 96dBA) but work in the United States discovered, contrary to expectations, that the hearing of a large sampling of musicians was not noticeably worse off for following their profession. Although still more research suggests that employees in recording studios and groups with 20 years experience suffer greater incidence of cardiac, gastrointestinal and circulatory problems than the general public. Again other work suggests that the younger generation are suffering progressive loss partially as a result of exposure to personal stereos (and therefore they require higher sound levels in performance).

Research at the University of Dresden suggests that studio engineers should limit themselves to the following amounts of exposure:

Table 5	MORE	
AVERAGE	SENSITIVE	TIME
85dBA	75dBA	1600 hrs (40 man weeks per year)
90dBA	80dBA	1000 hrs (25 man weeks per year)
95dBA	85dBA	500 hrs (12.5 man weeks per year)
100dBA	90dBA	280 hrs (7 man weeks per year)

Some licencing authorities have attempted to limit sound pressure level at concerts when granting licences, limits of 90 and 98dBA are typical. But in one concert at Wembley Stadium the system was so loud but so clear that the artist was able to apologise for the noise to those living nearby, whilst still in the middle of her act!

More recently at the new London Arena sound pressure level meters which are set to 110dB have been fitted underneath the roof, if the level of sound in the auditorium excedes this then a flashing light in the auditorium warns the operators, alternatively the system can be set so that the power cuts out and the process for its restoration is long.

On both sides of the Atlantic, legislation promises to impose some limits, and already there are several reports from the U.S.A. of legal action being brought by members of the audience against musicians as recompense for loss of

hearing apparently caused at concerts. In Europe the EEC regulations are required to be uniform by 1990 and this suggests that the U.K. will have more stringent industrial criteria applied.

A hand-held meter for measuring the sound pressure level at various frequencies.

In fact the new criteria do echo the tables above since in both the above cases exposure to a sound level of 90dBa (at 50m, 164' outdoors) is limited to 8 hours per day. The EEC regulations measure exposure also in 8 hour time limits (in units of dB LAeq) and above 90dB LAeq the regulations require that hearing protectors must be worn. If imposed this would have a dramatic effect on the disco and concert industry and at the time of writing there is some dialogue on an alternative approach. Obviously until conclusive research is available it is prudent to err on the side of safety and there are on the market several devices which can be set to cut off the power or sound an alarm at predetermined dB settings.

In sound system design outside the disco (where high sound levels are popular rather than necessary) sound levels can come down if the system delivers improved clarity. For example the author consulted on a replacement system for a large venue where the client wanted an average sound pressure level of 120dB based on the performance of his old system. The client was persuaded to accept 108dB but runs the new system at 80dB because of the improved clarity. We shall see later how this clarity can be calculated and used to influence the choice and location of the loudspeakers.

SUMMARY

Section One will be valuable as a reference throughout the book so it is worth summarising the basics.

The number of vibrations per second is known as the frequency which is expressed as Hz, the first vibration being the fundamental, subsequent multiple vibrations being harmonics. Music has a very wide frequency range, speech has a limited range. High frequency sounds are more directional than low frequency sounds.

The decibel is a unit of comparison between two other measurements – one of which may be an agreed standard reference.

The level of sound in auditoria is measured as sound pressure level – SPL – and is expressed as dB with 0dB being the agreed limit of hearing for reference at a frequency of 1000Hz, any SPL figure must mention the distance at which the measurement was taken.

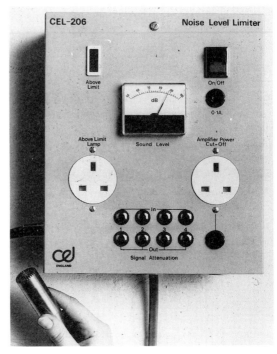

The CEL noise level limiter for monitoring and attenuating excessively loud entertainment noise.

SECTION TWO – ACOUSTICS

REVERBERATION

When a sound is produced in a large room, it can often continue to be heard for some time after the source has been cut off. This is the result of the sound bouncing round the walls of the room before reaching the listener and this process is known as reverberation. Just how much reverberation is heard at this point depends not only on the strength of the original sound but also on the size and shape of the room and upon how it is furnished.

Reverberation extends the effect of a single sound and whilst this might be desirable in music it is most certainly not so in speech, where the result will be blurred and unintelligible dialogue. Some sounds suffer more than others – vowels are especially liable to be obscured by the delay on preceding strong consonants. So we can see that an auditorium which has an ideal reverberation time (Rt) for music will not be ideal for speech, and vice-versa. Different forms of music require a different Rt – for example classical and modern music usually need a shorter Rt than choral work. So again even within the music spectrum, there are conflicting requirements for designers of multi-purpose auditoria.

Controlling the reverberation is therefore a fundamental of good acoustic design and it can be identified as the time (expressed as the Rt, or Rt60) that a point sound takes to die away by 60dB – otherwise to one millionth of its intensity (since an intensity of 60dB may be written as a ratio 1,000,000:1 or 10^6:1). In the case of existing buildings Rt is found by producing a point sound, typically a gun shot, but in the case of a proposed building the Rt has to be calculated.

This is done by considering the dimensions of the auditorium with respect to the amount of sound its surfaces will absorb. We will take a closer look at absorption later and especially at the influence that the audience has on sound. There are, in fact, several ways of calculating the Rt and the use of computers has led to the discovery that these formulae are not as accurate as was once thought. The discrepancies arise because the calculations' constant values are sometimes relatively inaccurate, and the more basic of the equations do not take into account the behaviour of sound waves nor the location of the different absorbing surfaces within the room.

The Rt differs at each frequency but if the measured frequency is not stated then it is assumed to be 500Hz. The capacity of the auditorium being measured is also important and should ideally be stated. If the seating is not absorbent a full auditorium can have an Rt as much as half a second lower than it did when it was empty. This overlooked fact has caused much dismay to musicians who often rehearse in empty halls. An auditorium possessing a long reverberation time is said to be 'lively' and a non-reverberant auditorium is said to be 'dead', recording studios often possess 'lively' and 'dead' areas for different uses.

Since a large auditorium is likely to have more reverberation than a small one a starting point in the case of the design of new buildings is the selection of the appropriate volume. This can itself be suggested by an average figure per seat. Whilst there is some dispute over the ideal figures the generally accepted volume per seat for music should be between 4.5 and 7.4 cubic metres (160 and 260 cubic feet) with 5.7 cubic metres as the best option (200 cubic feet). The figures for speech range from 2.3 to 4.3 cubic metres (80 to 150 cubic feet) with 3.1 cubic metres as the best option (110 cubic feet). The precise volume depends on the use, the kind of music involved and the balance with the amount of speech involved. (Once the volume is fixed the question of furnishing must be addressed,

Table 6

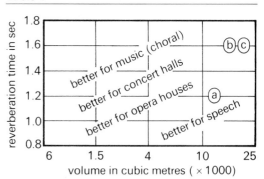

reverberation times with volume

a *Covent Garden Opera House 1.2 (12,240 cu m)*
b *Free Trade Hall, Manchester 1.6 (15,500 cu m)*
c *Royal Festival Hall, London 1.6 (22,000 cu m)*

soft furnishings absorb more frequencies than hard surfaces so less sound is reflected back into the auditorium; shortening the Rt.)

In simple terms we may summarise this section by saying that speech requires a less lively acoustic than music, and that electronic means aside, this may be achieved by introducing sound absorbing soft-furnishing elements into the auditorium – curtains, carpets, and people, being the easiest to obtain.

ELECTRO-ACOUSTIC REVERBERATION

It can be clearly seen therefore that, in purely architectural terms, the design of a good acoustic for multi-purpose use is extremly complex. Several post-war concert halls have an Rt shorter than was originally expected and have been obliged to resort to electronics to overcome the problem, there are two main systems employed – ambiophony – and assisted resonance.

Not surprisingly these systems are most often located in auditoria where music is the prime content. The most famous example of assisted resonance is the work of P.H. Parkin at the Royal Festival Hall. Other systems in the U.K. can be found at York University, Hexagon Centre Reading, the Beck Hillingdon, Dartford Orchard, Plymouth Royal and there are numerous examples on the continent.

The basic difference in the two systems is that ambiophony technique employs a few microphones placed close to the source of sound. These are then fed to delay units, usually produc-

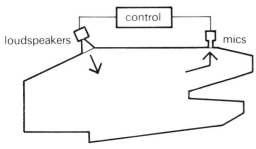

ASSISTED RESONANCE
A large quantity of carefully positioned microphones pick up the sound which is then filtered, delayed and amplified before passing to concealed loudspeakers thus extending the reverberation time.

ing four alternate times, relevant to the length of the auditorium – and thence to sets of loudspeakers positioned in the auditorium ceiling appropriate to the amount of delay given. Some reservations about this method have been expressed with regard to feedback generated by the close miking; critics claim that the system may suit some acoustics and presentations, but not all.

The assisted resonance system is more complex and one has to say, more expensive, consequently its critics claim that adoption in venues which do not present a high quantity of music might distort the use of limited funds. The assisted resonance system places numerous microphones stategically in the ceiling, mounted in specially resonant boxes. The sound is then filtered to emerge from many loudspeakers mounted again in the ceiling.

It is true that assisted resonance has its opponents who claim 'if a single capacitor or resistor blows up, the whole sound system is gone' and such critics are now working on increasing volumes within existing buildings rather than by relying on electronics. However it is also true that research is now being undertaken into utilising electronics to lower the Rt of a space, this technique closely resembles anti-phase systems used to silence electric motors and likely to appear elsewhere in the future, especially in aircraft.

Meanwhile at Delft in Holland a system has been installed into a concert hall which utilises computer simulation to offer various acoustics relative to the size of the orchestra and the type of music which it is playing.

Another system developed in Holland and now available in the U.K. is SIAP (System for Improved Acoustic Performance). Whilst this system can increase the Reverberation Time it also takes account of early and lateral reflections and therefore SIAP is also designed to enhance the sound quality.

REFLECTIONS AND REFLECTORS

Whenever a sound is produced in an auditorium whether it is a live one from actor or instrument, or an amplified one via a loudspeaker, a certain portion of the sound will not reach the audience directly but will be reflected from the walls, ceilings and other surfaces in the auditorium.

Just as the reverberation time can be harmful or useful, so the reflections need careful control. Reflections can be harmful where they arrive at the listener after the direct sound and blur the words, or they may be useful where they combine with the direct sound to improve volume and intelligibility, the first reflection (arriving within 10ms of the direct sound) is particularly important in this respect. In the case of music because the orchestra will most certainly be located in the same place each time (in respect to the audience) the design is easier than for speech where the actor/lecturer/audience relationship can alter and this makes the use of reflected sound more difficult.

It is possible to determine what reflections will be produced by sounds striking different surfaces. Consider a concave surface, such as domes, circle fronts and rear walls of auditoria. There the sound is concentrated by the surface,

and reflected often with equal intensity so that some people could experience a blurring of the original sound and even a distinct echo.

The most famous example of this phenomenon is the Royal Albert Hall dome, where the severe echos were somewhat overcome by the suspension of 'flying saucers' to prevent the direct sound reaching the concave surface of the dome itself. This is perhaps an extreme example but it serves to illustrate the point. In most situations the culprit is more likely to be a curved rear wall or circle fascia. The radius of the curve will determine where the reflected sound is concentrated and it may be that the artists on stage suffer more than the audience. In this case the problem should not be dismissed merely because the paying patrons are not directly affected. They will be indirectly affected by the result of the sound on the performer, the focal point of any curve must lie outside not only the audience but the stage area too.

One aspect of the concave shape which has to

The Royal Albert Hall showing the 'flying saucers' which prevent much sound from reaching the dome and causing an echo ... note also the centre loudspeaker cluster.

be considered is the radius of the curve and its relationship to wavelength. The distance across the arc gives a direct indication of the frequencies affected. For example an untreated curved back wall with a radius of 20m (65.5') will focus sounds down the range – provided that it is not obstructed by balconies nor covered with heavy absorbent material. Even if it is obstructed it may still reflect high frequency sounds. The same principle applies to small arcs like ceiling cornices and balcony fronts which reflect only high frequency sounds.

Rectangular rooms can produce a number of problems. In particular, corner reflections occur where the sound hits the ceiling, or the underside of a balcony, and is reflected back towards the audience via the rear wall. This problem is par-

ticularly acute with the high frequency (short wavelength) sounds and wall or ceiling treatment is again desirable to absorb or disperse the sound.

Parallel walls can cause 'flutter echoes' which greatly impede intelligibility. The echoes are caused by audience sounds, coughing and programme rustling, bouncing back and forth across the auditorium without any chance of being dispersed. Ideally the walls should be slightly angled so that the audiences' sound path is dispersed towards the rear of the auditorium and the reflected programme sound can also be dispersed to reinforce the direct sound path. In an existing building the problem can be overcome by providing a more absorbent wall surface, although of course this will alter the reverberation time. Another method is to attach panels to the wall which are each at a slight angle

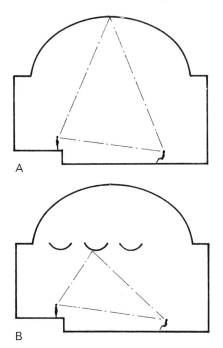

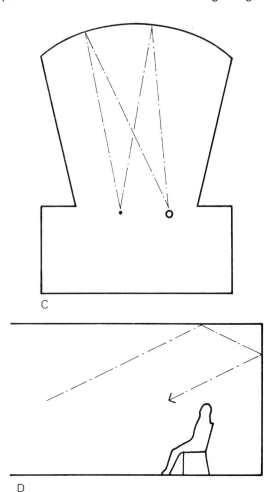

HARMFUL REFLECTIONS
In A the sound can reach the dome and be refocussed back to the audience with such a delay that it is heard as an echo. In B convex ceiling reflectors have been hung and these prevent the sound reaching the dome and help it to be reflected usefully. A similar problem occurs in C where the curved rear wall acts as a reflector, this time harming the actors on stage. Right angles as in D can also re-focus sounds in disturbing ways; in both C and D some acoustic treatment for the walls is needed.

to the main surface and which can themselves be made more absorbent. These act as small reflectors, again dispersing the sound towards the rear.

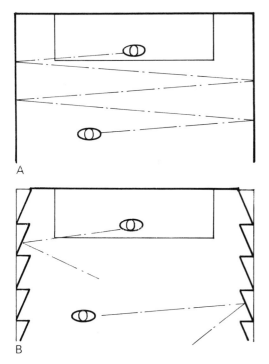

FLUTTER ECHOES

In A the hard parallel side walls cause any audience sound to bounce back and forth but in B reflectors have been placed to overcome this and to help aim the side reflections from the platform further down the hall. This is in fact a solution which the author applied to a specific building, the fact that the reflectors were pronounced in this way enabled house lighting and stage lighting to be concealed although the echoes would be reduced with a shallower treatment.

Another kind of reflection frequently found in rectangular or parallel areas is that of standing waves. As we saw earlier these are accentuations of certain frequencies whose wavelength is an exact multiple of one of the auditorium's basic dimensions. The accent is placed on a frequency only in parts of the auditorium but (apart from discomforting the audience) this can give rise to feedback if a microphone needs to be placed in that position because the sound system then becomes more sensitive to the frequency which is being emphasised. One solution is to insert a precision filter (called a notch filter) into the

sound chain to de-emphasise the prominent frequency. This may have to be done several times (with a device called a graphic equaliser) and we shall look at this process in more detail later. Another aid is to make the surfaces more absorbent to cut down the reflection.

Parallel walls are often the easiest design option and it should be noted that many of the world's greatest concert halls are or were rectangular, so once again the building designer must have a clear brief as to the use.

Convex surfaces will disperse the sound and this may prove helpful if the dispersal can reinforce the direct non-reflected sound waves. This is the basic principal behind the reflectors often seen above concert platforms or modern theatre orchestra pits. The size of the reflector is important because it relates to the wavelength of the sounds involved. It is of no value merely to fix the size in relationship to what looks good, the dimensions of the reflector must relate to the wavelength of the frequencies involved. A significantly small dimension (less than 17' (5.4m) where full music reproduction is needed) would cause the sound to bend round the edge and not as much will be reflected (it must be clear that a certain amount of this bending – known as edge diffraction – is inevitable anyway in view of the long wavelengths of the extreme lower frequencies). Since speech has higher fundamentals and therefore smaller wavelengths the dimension could be reduced if necessary in speech-only systems but this would be unwise since venues have a nasty habit of changing their function during their lifetime!

Ideally the reflector board should be removable or should at least have removable panels. There are two reasons for this. First, modern pit orchestras often possess electronic instruments which their owners choose to excessively amplify (often incorrectly) in the pit itself. Not only does this produce an unbalanced sound by comparison with more traditional instruments but also the amplified sound is focussed by the reflector board above into the auditorium producing an even greater level from the orchestra as a whole over which the vocal mics have to climb. Secondly multi-purpose venues require a variety of equipment to be hung in front of the proscenium and access within the reflector board is required for touring lighting and sound trusses.

The Royal Festival Hall showing the tiers of reflector panels above the platform.

The auditorium therefore has to be carefully designed so that the reflected sound in all areas is either helpful to the main sound or is absorbed. Convex surfaces are useful to disperse and reflect desirable sounds, concave surfaces may lead to harmful echoes and parallel surfaces are to be avoided where speech intelligibility is of paramount importance.

THE GRAZING EFFECT – SEATING LAYOUT

Earlier we saw how the sound level decreased 6dB every time the distance away from the source was doubled. We also know that reflected sounds can be harmful to intelligibility therefore the closer that the audience are to the stage then the better they should hear, because the direct sound will not have so far to travel and the first order reflections can be better utilised.

Much of the strength of the sound is being absorbed by the audience as it passes over their heads (the grazing effect) and one way to overcome this is to remove the obstruction – raise each row above the previous on the tiered or raking principle. All rear rows will need a higher tier or angle of rake than those in front to preserve the benefit, and the circle and balcony levels will need the highest increase that is permissible under the licensing regulations.

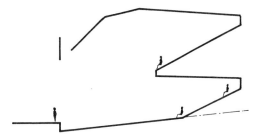

RAKED SEATING
The dotted line shows how the rear seats would have been placed if their rows had not been inclined more steeply. This is one way to improve both sight lines and hearing for seating a long way from the stage. Such steep seating would be stepped rather than raked.

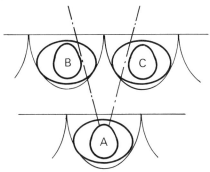

STAGGERED SEATING
A can see and hear better if his row is adjusted so that his seat is centred between those of B and C. Although this method lowers capacity slightly it improves audience ambience.

The sightlines are also improved by this method and ideally the seats should be staggered so that one person looks between the heads of those in front. The rows should also be curved so that the natural focus of each seat is the centre of the performing area. Regrettably retractable seating is often all that can be afforded, sentencing many patrons on the ends of rows to twist uncomfortably in their seats; retractable seating tiers are often also quite noisy as people enter late or leave early. Curved rows and staggered seating are not popular because they are both expensive and more difficult than straight rows to fit into a design. This is especially true of multi-purpose auditoria where the stalls floor often has to be flat to cater for sports, dances and exhibitions. Ideally great consideration should be given to the provision of either rostra with traditional seating or air-caster seating for the rear rows where the effect of distance and absorption will be most felt.

Retractable seating which provides versatility and improves both sightlines and hearing for the rear rows.

INSULATION AND ABSORPTION

These two terms are often confused with each other so we will define them first.

ABSORPTION

Sound Absorption is the term used to cover the process whereby the surfaces of the auditorium can be treated to reflect different amounts of sound at different frequencies. The amount of absorption has a direct bearing on the reverberation and you may remember that we have said that generally hard surfaces reflect (do not absorb) as much sound as soft surfaces. Sound Insulation is the term used to cover the process of preventing sound from one area intruding into another and the most effective kind of insulation is weight, a real sound-proof door is heavy!

There is an incorrect but often repeated theory that sound absorbing tiles will prevent sound from being passed from one area to another. The tiles will certainly help to reduce the reverberation in one area and thus limit the amount of sound likely to pass into the other area, but only proper insulation will really be effective.

The amount of absorption present in a room can be measured and forms a fundamental part of the Reverberation time (Rt) calculation. There are several equations but the most commonly known formula is that developed by W.C. Sabine in the late 19th century is:

$$\text{Reverberation Time} = \frac{0.16\ (constant) \times volume\ m^3}{total\ absorbtion\ in\ m^2\ sabin\ units}$$

The sabin is a unit of absorption and values are available for building and furnishing materials. Were the absorption to be total then the coefficient would be 1 and conversely were no sound to be absorbed then the value would be 0. Here are some common values:

Table 7
ABSORPTION COEFFICIENTS

	250Hz	500Hz	1000Hz
Brickwork	0.04	0.02	0.04
Concrete	0.02	0.02	0.04
Plaster solid backing	0.03	0.02	0.03
Carpet, thick pile	0.25	0.5	0.5
Air (per m³)	nil	nil	0.003
Audience in seat upholstered	0.4	0.46	0.46
Wooden seat, empty		0.15	
Rostrum per m²	0.1	nil	nil

It should be noted that materials have in fact several frequency bands of coefficients since the absorption varies with frequency. Typically the measurements for each material are taken at 125Hz, 250Hz, 400Hz, 1000Hz and 4000Hz; the figures shown above are in simpler form for illustration rather than for the basis of calculations. It is also worth noting that there is no definitive table of absorption coefficients since different acousticians and laboratories have used varying techniques to achieve measurements. The differences however are slight.

The above formula is altered where the calculations involve large auditoria and where the air has an absorption factor too. The formula then appears thus:

$$\text{Reverberation Time} = \frac{0.16\ (constant) \times volume\ m^3}{Absorption\ m^2\ sabins + XV}$$

Where **V** is room volume in m³
X is air coefficient

Where imperial measurements are involved the constant changes thus:

$$\text{Reverberation Time} = \frac{0.05\ (constant) \times volume\ in\ feet^3}{Absorption\ in\ feed^2\ sabins \times volume \times air\ coefficient}$$

Acoustic model of the (ill-fated) Edinburgh Opera House built to one-eighth scale in 1975, today the model could be made smaller or the acoustics could even be tested on computer.

The use of computers in acoustics has determined that the Sabine formula is not as accurate as was once thought since it does not take into account either the location of the various absorbing surfaces in the auditorium or the way in which sound is diffused. (There is a more recent equation – the Fitzroy formula, for use where the absorption is not distributed evenly and in this case the calculation is carried out for each axis of the room and the result added.)

In a high performance building, such as a concert hall, any error in the calculation of the Rt, and in the placing of reflectors and absorbers is critical and it is interesting to note what work is being done to reduce this error. One way is to produce a scaled down model of the theatre accurate in every detail and capable of behaving acoustically as a small version of the real thing. Acoustic tests are carried out and the results scaled up accordingly. Until recently this has been very expensive and thus only justifiable for high performance areas. However research carried out in England has reduced this cost considerably by working to smaller scales. For example the ill fated Edinburgh Opera House model was costed in 1975 at £12,000 and built to a scale of 1/8. Five years later the models were scaled at 1/50 and cost only £4,000. Since then the use of computers has extended progress even further so that a combination of acoustic calculation programs and Computer Aided Design systems often mean that structural models are not required at all.

Returning to absorption it can be seen from Table 7 that hard surfaces absorb less sound than soft surfaces and hence they are good reflectors. For example at 500Hz brick, concrete or plaster absorbs only 2% of the sound whereas carpet absorbs 50%. The thickness of the surface is important, especially with soft furnishing such as carpets; thin felt on concrete absorbs only 25% at 500Hz, whereas thick pile on concrete absorbs 50% at the same frequency. Hence it is possible to achieve some comfort in the furnishing without seriously lowering the Rt.

More absorption is achieved if a substance, say timber slats or curtain, is placed some distance away from the wall so that an air gap is formed. The actual distance is critical, a gap of $1\frac{1}{2}''$ provides up to 10dB less absorption at 500Hz than does a gap of 6". Similarly the choice of curtain material itself is important, a relatively open weave is better at absorbing sound than a heavy material because the sound loses energy passing through the curtain.

Should this principal be taken further so that individual cavities are formed – called Helmholtz resonators – then specific frequencies can be absorbed very well although others in the range are not, so these cavities are useful for dealing with troublesome frequencies.

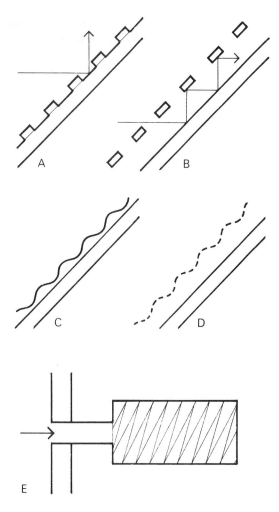

WALL TREATMENTS

The timber slats in B are absorbing more sound than in A because the sound is losing energy in the gaps. Similarly the thinner curtain D is more absorbent than the thick curtain C for the same reason. E shows a specifically designed port and absorbent, tuned to trap a particular frequency, this device is known as a Helmholtz resonator.

The treatment of the wall surface itself is also important, for example a porous brick surface can have its absorption lowered by 20% by one coat of paint applied with roller, or raised by 15% if one coat is applied by brush. (These figures at 500Hz.)

From the above it can be seen that the reverberation time can be adjusted by introducing or eliminating absorbent surfaces into the auditorium. However it should be noted that for each 3dB adjustment in reverberant sound the absorption has to alter by a factor of 2. Generally the Rt is too long and doubling the amount of soft furnishing might not be impossible in a multi-purpose hall but it would be a challenge in a traditional plush-and-gilt theatre. The Rt can also be adjusted by altering the volume of the auditorium and although most managers would rather not reduce capacity permanently several theatres now have sliding walls or lowering ceilings.

INSULATION

In the past insulation was generally confined to the prevention of undesirable sounds from reaching the auditorium, perhaps from a neighbouring factory, road or railway. The basic premise of good design here is to create a double shell building, the Royal Festival Hall being an early and excellent example, sited as it is next to a major railway line. (However more recently the growth and power of rock-music frequently now means that auditorium must be designed to contain the sound and prevent it annoying the neighbours!)

Another basic premise is that in insulation the 'weak link' theory predominates again – for example, a thick wall will be far less effective if penetrated by doors and windows. If the windows or doors are not in use then they should be bricked up – simple boarding is not sufficient though some slight improvement would occur.

Any membrane, such as a door, wall or window, effects some reduction to the level of sound passing through it, and since this can be calculated, it is possible to indicate how thick a membrane should be, and of what it should be constructed in order to achieve the desired reduction. The actual amount of reduction varies with the frequency but for an example, a standard 4" (100mm) brick wall with plaster both sides, effects a reduction of about 40dB. Therefore if the theatre is encompassed by such walls and the sound pressure level attendant on the theatre side of the wall is say 80dB then the sound pressure level on the other side will be about 40dB (there are many other aspects to be counted here such as the positions of windows, doors, air-trunking and the way in which the sound is generated and also its frequency but nevertheless these figures can be used for guidance). A table of other membranes and their reduction indices is given in the appendix.

If doors and windows are in use then only acoustically designed units will make any attempt to preserve the benefit of the heavy wall. In the case of windows a fixed frame will be a better insulator than an opening one and, of course, double glazing also helps a great deal although the air gap should be at least 200mm for there to be any benefit. Heavier glass, more panes and a greater air gap is still better, a 10mm pane, 200mm gap and 8mm pane providing 52dB of insulation, more than a 250mm cavity brick wall. Doors should be examined to ensure that they close properly – gaps can let through much sound, but the only real solution is an air lock.

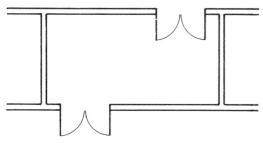

AIR LOCKS
However thick the walls are around a building the sound will always escape or enter through weak points, doors and windows. Double doors, offset as shown here help to overcome this.

Areas surrounding the main auditorium should be as absorbent as possible and provided with carpets and curtains to cut down the reverberant sound – curtains are especially useful anyway to improve decor and carpets help cushion the impact sound (from high heels for example) which travels through the structure.

In heating and ventilation systems the general principle is that the noise near a duct or grille is substantially higher than elsewhere so all grilles should be placed well away from the audience. A common problem occurs when the use of a theatre changes, requiring a lower background noise level than that which was acceptable when the building originally opened. Under these circumstances it is not realistic to install a new heating and ventilation system and hence the answer is usually to fit silencers to the grilles and perhaps in extreme cases lower the speed of the system. Some people even switch it off altogether during the actual curtain up times, using it only before the show and during the interval but consideration needs to be given to the needs of the licence which requires a certain number of changes of air per hour.

To summarise – insulation deals with preventing sound being transmitted and is best achieved by weight. Absorption deals with the reflection of sound by the design of surfaces and is based on the fact that different substances absorb different amounts of sound at various frequencies.

THE ORCHESTRA AREA

Where any work involves the contribution of several orchestral players, be it opera, concert or light entertainment, it is fundamental that the area housing those players must receive careful consideration. We shall deal with two types – the stage performance by an orchestra and the orchestra pit.

Earlier we talked of a given reverberation time being more suitable for one kind of music than another and there is a direct parallel in the orchestra pit. The Italian opera houses favoured for Mozartian opera have large open orchestra pits and this is ideal for small orchestras and in well orchestrated works where the singers are not overpowered. However a large orchestra, such as that required for Wagner, may indeed be too loud by comparison with the singers if left completely in the open. The solution therefore is to partially enclose the pit by placing some of it

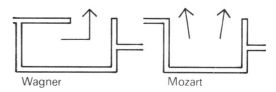

Wagner   Mozart

ORCHESTRA PITS
The Wagner pit tends to blend sound and ease the balance between musician and singer, it also permits the stage to be nearer to front row. The Mozart pit gives equal rein to all the sound.

under the stage. This is believed to have been introduced by Wagner himself at the opera house he designed at Bayreuth.

In more recent times, musicals such as 'Jesus Christ Superstar' totally enclosed the pit in perspex so that the sound was completely under the control of the sound engineer through microphones on each instrument. This technique enabled not only the balance of one instrument against another to be controlled, but also the volume. It must be appreciated that under these cicumstances the conductor is denied much control over the final balance yet techniques like this are often employed with works conceived in studios or popularised by recordings.

Generally then, the pit should be large enough to accomodate many players. If opera and ballet are envisaged this might mean at least 60 musicians but for most light entertainment work 30 would be a maximum. It has been suggested that a player should be accomodated within between 1m² and 1.5m². The pit should be designed to blend the sound in the correct balance with the sound of the performers on stage. It is advisable to plan for later additions of acoustic treatment to the walls and ceiling – it is easier to add panels later than to take them away, although acoustics that would please one musician are unlikely to please another! The sightlines from musician to conductor are important, and lifts (combined with rostra) are useful.

Of course for many people an orchestra pit is a luxury and they have to content themselves with fencing off part of the auditorium floor. This introduces two dangers: first, the pit as a whole is now higher than normal and might intrude into the sightlines of the stalls. Secondly the whole orchestra is now clearly into the acoustic of the audience and could well have more prominence than the performers on stage who have few reflectors to help them. Many complaints of bands being too loud occur in this situation.

The solution is obviously not easy, short of physical alterations. The pit itself, floor and walls should be lined with as much absorbent material as possible. Trial and error will tell which areas need more than others – brass and timpani are certainly candidates and almost certainly no amplification should be employed except perhaps for the strings. Alternatively, the production

might allow for the orchestra to be placed on stage, where there are more absorbents, although care needs to be taken with performers' mics picking up the instruments.

In more serious works such as concerts the orchestra are always on stage. Since we are concerned with theatre we will not deal here with the design of the concert platform. However when theatres and multi-purpose halls stage concerts the central problem is that of absorption. Placed on stage among drapes and scenery the reverberation time is lower, and much is lost to the cavernous fly tower above. The requirement is to make the stage acoustic at one with the auditorium. The orchestra should be as far downstage as possible and obviously an apron (possibly an orchestra pit lift) is a distinct advantage here. Next, the rear musicians should be mounted on rostra to improve sightlines and hearing for those at the back of the hall. Attractive though it may be, as far as possible there should be no curtaining involved.

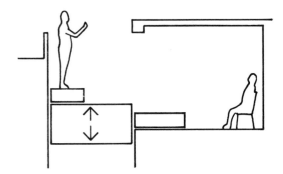

PIT LIFTS
A pit lift not only allows the conductor more control over the height of the musicians, backed up by rostra, but also doubles as an apron stage and a method of transporting loads under the stage for storeage.

If the event is frequent, it would be worth investing in a series of hard reflector flats to form a band 'shell'. The construction of the flats is important since unless they are able to form a wall and not remain as separate units then only some frequencies will be reflected – notably the higher ones. The surface should be hardboard or ply – not canvas. Ceiling pieces are easily dealt with in theatres with fly-towers and it is conceivable that the units could be permanently rigged

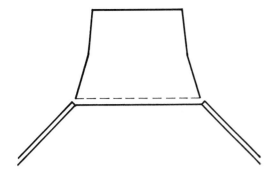

BAND SHELLS
When the orchestra are on stage it is necessary to prevent the sound from being absorbed in the fly tower. Band shells consist of what is effectively a box set of hard walls and ceiling and some small stages have a complete unit which unfolds, often stored on the back wall or flown in via motors.

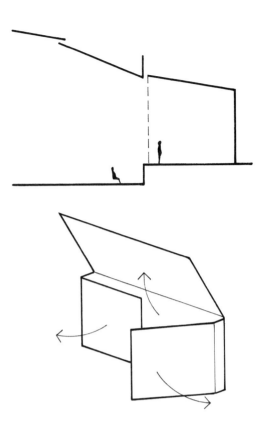

and just dropped in as required, provided that not too many flying lines are taken up. Theatres without flying facilities are not likely to suffer much from the loss of ceiling pieces as there will be no fly tower and there will therefore be less volume to damage the reverberation time, although the reflections will still be lost of course. If the band shell units are positioned with care and painted the same colour as the auditorium – the illusion of one room, as well as of one acoustic, will be improved. However one should note that few band shells are successful, not for any particular acoustic reasons but because they take up too much storage space, too many flying lines in the grid or are too time consuming to erect.

There are other aspects of orchestral work involving equipment which we will look at later. Meanwhile, let us summarise by saying that the orchestral area is not a backstage facility which can be ignored; it requires as much consideration as the performance itself.

AUDITORIUM SHAPE

Now that we know more of the behaviour of sound waves in a room we are able to discuss the ideal auditorium shape before going on to some more detailed aspects of sound system design.

We saw earlier that the rectangular shape was very popular with designers of concert halls – Boston Symphony Hall, Bristol Colston Hall, Vienna Musikvereinssaal, Glasgow St. Andrews Hall, to select just four. They have been considered to have the most desirable qualities for music with respect to the dispersion of direct and indirect sound and the sense of involvement created for the audience. The rectangular shape also had historic social connections with parts of the audience being more desirous of seeing each other than of the stage or platform.

There may be some confusion arising in the reader's mind since we have spoken of the need to avoid parallel surfaces which create flutter echoes and standing waves, but it must be remembered that these buildings are often richly decorated in a way that sound is therefore either dispersed or absorbed. The architect's vocabulary is smaller today than it was last century as far as interior structural decor is concerned and large plain surfaces proliferated especially in venues built in the 1960s. However today the boxes and

The Towngate Theatre Basildon . . . a new theatre re-affirming the old auditorium format.

circle slips have made a comeback producing not only a livelier auditorium but also some useful dispersion. Nevertheless parallel walls remain useful in pure music areas since they can add fullness to the sound by the wave patterns they help to create, but they should be chosen by the acoustic consultant and architect specifically with that in mind, rather than adopted as the easiest construction option.

One disadvantage of the rectangular concert hall is the flat floor which increases the absorption of sound over the heads of the audience so that back rows often have difficulty in hearing. The reason for the choice of floor is that concert halls were frequently multi-purpose and also housed dancing and banquets: something many

managers of today will understand. The benefits to the box office of multi-purpose are often achieved at the expense of the integral nature of each form of entertainment. Compromise often makes an audience uneasy and performers may have to work harder to compensate.

However one compromise which has been proven to work in stalls seating is that of combining a flat stalls floor for the first half of the seating and then tiering the remainder – often in phases which have been referred to as vineyard steps. In this form the flat seating is sufficiently close to the stage for the grazing effect to be negligible whilst the tiering at the rear not only improves the acoustics for the audience but the sightlines as well. People have stated that they feel closer to the stage if they can see clearly above the heads of those in front.

VINEYARD STEPS
For multipurpose buildings a flat floor is essential but this prevents the rear rows from having good sightlines, stepped seating is often the answer.

For multi-purpose auditoria, it is not un-reasonable to suggest that the flat floor could be provided with removable seating (preferably in curved rows on air-casters) whilst the tiering could be permanent or rostra (with retractable as a last resort).

In large capacity venues it is better to form an arena – using well tiered rear rows – than to build a large box. Many theatres are constructed on the fan shaped principle in order to position as many people as possible close to the stage. But this is not a twentieth century idea since the Greeks built Epidaurus this way about 300BC. The design is interesting since it suggests the Greeks knew a lot about acoustics – consider the tiering which overcomes the grazing effect for example, and which of course provides excellent sightlines.

The Greek theatre at Epidaurus showing the orchestra reflector, steep tiering and fan shape layout.

In large auditoria in order to preserve good tiering in the stalls, a balcony may become too steep and in any case the overhang will shorten the reverberation of the sound to the rear stalls as well as making them feel shut off from other parts of the auditorium. Unfortunately a balcony is essential with very large seating capacities otherwise the back row of the arena would be too far away, a recent compromise is to provide a number of small balconies where the projection is kept to a minimum.

The National Theatre of Taiwan showing the shallow tiers which permit good sightlines and acoustics for those below.

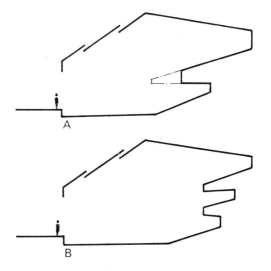

BALCONY SHADOW
The theatre in B has the same capacity as A but the sightlines and acoustics for the rear rows are much better because they are not shadowed by the overhand of the circle.

We may summarise by saying that orchestral needs are traditionally served by rectangular arenas (the parallel walls can add fullness to the tone but need careful design to avoid flutter echoes). Larger capacities than could be reasonably accommodated in a rectangular hall could be met by a fan shape or by adding a balcony, though both cause problems; fan shapes tend to introduce harmful concave surfaces and balconies inhibit the stalls tiering which benefits both sightlines and acoustics. Speech is better in well-absorbed fan-shaped auditoria than in rectangular auditoria, because of the shorter reverberation times and the inherent shape which aids useful reflections.

A Matcham auditorium (here restored at the Theatre Royal Newcastle) and typical of his compact elegant and excellent acoustical designs.

STRUCTURAL ALTERATIONS

Structural improvements to either an auditorium or stage are rare once a building has opened but redecoration is not unknown. In any event the excitement at securing sufficient funds should not obscure the fact that the acoustics could change.

Often drapes that were thought merely decorative are removed resulting in an increase in the Rt, or they are added and the room becomes deader. Lighting slots are cut into ceiling or walls, which adds the volume of the void to that of the main auditorium, increasing the Rt at certain frequencies. If this does happen it is also important that the Rt of the void is less than that of the main auditorium otherwise sound will be heard to reverberate in the void after it has died away in the auditorium. Another problem in the introduction of a void area next to the auditorium is that some insulation will be lost between the auditorium and the adjacent area – the weak link now being the slot itself and the double skin construction being pierced.

On very rare occasions, massive alterations may take place, like extending the balcony or adding a fly-tower, with consequent massive changes in volume and Rt. Studies have shown that a fly-tower without absorbent material can add over a second to the reverberation time at lower frequencies.

Sometimes scenery is brought out onto apron walls and ceilings, transforming what was once a carefully designed reflector into an absorber.

On all such occasions the acoustics will change – possibly for the better – but consideration of the result should be made first.

SECTION THREE –EQUIPMENT

cont. overleaf

THE ITEMS IN THE CHAIN

Now we come to the most important part of the chain – the equipment itself – and nowhere is the concept of a chain more relevant. It is vital that all items are of compatible standard. They must match not only electrically but qualitatively. For example the purchase of an expensive microphone will be largely wasted if there is an item further down the chain which is inferior, because it will inhibit the benefit of the microphone. Quite often the inferior items are the loudspeakers and of course we should not forget that positioning and operating these devices is part of the chain too, a good loudspeaker is useless unless well positioned, and we will look at this later. Often a complete system is too expensive to be purchased at one time and the venue must resort to a phased programme. This is acceptable, as long as the final goal is still kept in sight and no-one is allowed to call a halt halfway. Frequently this is not explained to ruling committees, whose response often is 'what do you want new loudspeakers for – we spent £4000 on a new mixer last year'.

In this section we will deal with each piece of equipment in detail, but first let us define the components of the chain.

THE MICROPHONE

This device picks up the sound. It can either be very selective, hearing activity immediately in front or not selective at all in which case it hears activity all around. Vocal microphones are usually cylindrical and either held in the performer's hand or mounted on a special stand, some designs can be fitted to radio transmitters to avoid trailing cables; alternative designs (called boundary mics) are mounted on a flat plate for general pickup and concealment on stage or in instruments. All microphones produce only a

A typical moving coil dynamic hand-held mic.

small electric current (which is in proportion to the fluctuations of the original sound waves) and the electrical signal is then passed to the Mixer.

THE MIXER

All the input signals from the microphones, and from recording devices such as reel-to-reel tape decks, record decks, cartridge, cassette and compact disc players (and sometimes from other mixers) are routed to the main mixer where each sound source is provided with its own control channel. Some mixers are very sophisticated, having as many as 30 different control functions per input channel, others are more basic and offer a simple volume control. It is here at the mixer that the different signals are processed, one volume balanced against another volume, and the tone (equalisation) adjusted. Finally, the signals are arranged in groups, each with its own master fader, perhaps relevant to either the geography of the theatre (stalls, circle) or to members of the production (orchestra, lead vocals) before passing to the Equaliser.

A typical small mixer, this one can be mounted in an equipment rack; note also the inbuilt graphic equaliser.

THE EQUALISER

This device is an optional extra and systems can exist with out its employment but its inclusion can greatly enhance the quality of the sound. The equaliser is a network of filters which allows for the adjustment of a large number of frequencies, usually at one-third octave intervals, right throughout the audio spectrum. The adjustments are made to level out any peaks or troughs created in the sound system's response to the

A parametric equaliser.

acoustics of the building. A system which is evened out in this way is said to be flatter and a flatter response from a sound system will mean more gain or volume before feedback (howl-round) occurs. The equaliser can also be used to enhance the quality of the sound, perhaps giving it more presence in the vital middle vocal frequencies. The signal then passes to the Amplifier.

THE AMPLIFIER

Up to now the signals have not been powerful enough to produce the drive and volume we require at the loudspeaker. The amplifier produces this power and leaves the signal otherwise unaltered passing it along to the last item in the chain.

THE LOUDSPEAKER

This unit works in the reverse way to the microphone. The electrical signals interact with a magnet fitted to the loudspeaker cone and this causes the cone to radiate sound waves in proportion to the original sound picked up by the microphone. There are many different kinds of loudspeakers – some units handle all the signal so that their design is by nature a compromise by comparison to other loudspeakers which handle only a part and therefore their design can be better suited to reproduce just that section of the audio signal. Some loudspeakers are constructed in vertical lines, called line sources, but most follow the point source format in which case their sound level observes the inverse square rule that their sound pressure level falls 6dB with every doubling of the distance.

A selection of amplifiers in various power ratings.

A popular wide range loudspeaker, this unit provides a constant directivity beam.

Such are the basic parts of a system. There are others that we will refer to later, delay lines, echo units, compressor limiters, monitors, tape units, disc units and the all-important wiring.

Now we will deal with each item in more detail.

MICROPHONES

As we have seen earlier, when vocal chords vibrate or musical instruments are played they cause waves of compression in the air proportionate to the fluctuations of the original sound. All microphones are fitted with a plate, known as a diaphragm, which receives the compression waves and then vibrates accordingly. From here there are two basic ways in which these vibrations may be converted into an electrical signal, and microphones are often referred to by the names of these two processes – dynamic or condenser.

Note that whilst all microphones follow the basic principle we are dealing with the types most suited to theatre working.

DYNAMIC MOVING-COIL

Probably the most common microphone around is the dynamic moving-coil microphone. Here the diaphragm is attached to a coil of wire which moves with it and which is suspended inside the poles of a magnet. As the diaphragm and coil move so the lines of force of the magnet are 'cut' by the coil, inducing an electrical signal propor-

tionate to the vibrations acting on the diaphragm.

These mics are among the oldest types (first appearing in the early 1920s) and are probably the most robust and also the most economical, a point to remember when dealing with some performers – or when mics have to be handed to the audience. A good quality dynamic moving-coil mic will give a good strong signal and can cover a wide range of frequencies without much deviation.

A selection of dynamic microphones; note that all are fitted with a metal grille 'pop-gag'.

CONDENSER

A condenser, or a capacitor as it is sometimes called, is found in many electronic devices. It has been defined as having the ability of facing conducting-surfaces to store an electric charge. In the condenser mic, one of the facing surfaces is fixed and supplied with a small electric charge.

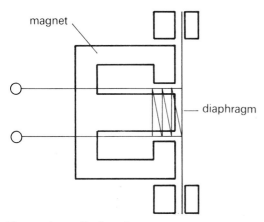

The moving coil microphone

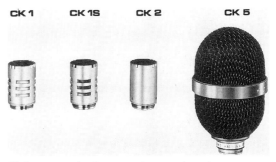

Pickup capsules for a condenser microphone system; CK1 is the normal unidirectional capsule, CK1S is a condenser with presence rise, CK2 is an omni-directional capsule and CK5 is the CK1 with a pop-gag fitted. (AKG C451 system).

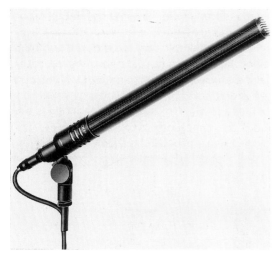

Condenser short rifle pickup tube (CK8).

The diaphragm forms the other surface and so movement of the diaphragm by the air waves causes vibrations in the charge proportionate to the original vibrations. All condenser microphones require a power supply unit to provide the initial charge, unless such a charge is supplied by a power source within the sound mixer and fed down the mic line. This process is known as phantom powering. Although there is some uniformity, not all condenser microphones work to the same charge so some careful checking is necessary, the common values are from 9 to 52v.

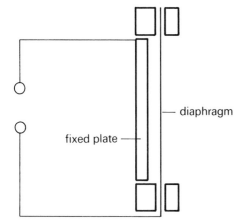

The condenser microphone

A more recent development in condenser mics is the electret mic where the capacitor is given a charge when the microphone is manufactured and since the capacitor will retain its charge indefinitely electret mics require no power supply.

Condenser microphones produce excellent results and are usually of better quality than moving coil microphones. They are very sensitive and usually have a very flat, even response over the whole audio spectrum (unlike electrets which can produce less LF and HF response – closer to the response of dynamics). For these reasons they have become a standard in recording and broadcasting.

PRESSURE AND PRESSURE GRADIENT MICS

In the pressure operated mic the sound waves act only on the front of the microphone – on one side of the diaphragm. In the pressure gradient mic the waves have access to both sides of the diaphragm. Since this is not possible simultaneously from one source – the waves arriving at the front before they arrive at the rear, various effects are possible and most pressure gradient mics emphasise the bass when used close to the performer's mouth, this may or may not be desirable.

In practical theatre usage, the terms 'pressure' and 'pressure gradient' are rarely used and microphones are referred to by the catalogue number of the manufacturer.

POLAR DIAGRAM, PICKUP, AXIS/OFF AXIS RESPONSE

A microphone that is sensitive on all sides is known as omnidirectional, these are rarely used as hand-held mics in theatre (because they can be sensitive to feedback) but are commonly associated with the concealed microphones used with radio transmitters in costume productions. If feedback occurs under these circumstances than small concealed cardioid capsules can be connected to the transmitter as an alternative. The polar diagram for omnidirectional mics is shown at the top of the next column.

One microphone occasionally found in the theatre is the ribbon mic. In this design a strip of corrugated foil is mounted on a coil placed between the poles a magnet. Fluctuations in the movement of the 'ribbon' will induce a current proportionate to the original vibrations. However not only is the ribbon fragile but also ribbon

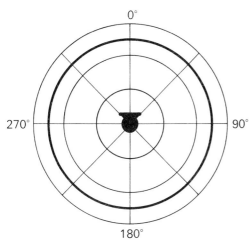

An omnidirectional polar diagram – sensitive on all sides

(It is worth noting that since the ribbon mic is sensitive only on the front and rear of the ribbon, not at the sides this mic is useful for recording vocal groups since several people can congregate easily and those not speaking can step to the sides 'off mic'.)

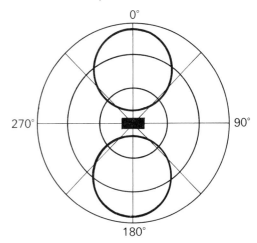

The figure of eight pickup of the ribbon mic – sensitive at 0° and 180° but not at 90° or 270°.

mics are sensitive on both sides of the ribbon which means that in theatre usage they will pickup sounds on both sides of the mic, the performer and the audience, pit orchestra and possibly the loudspeakers too. As with the omnidirectional mic this is unacceptable too because not only do we want to avoid feedback or howlround but we also want to life the performer above the sound produced by the orchestra and the other performers and to do that the microphone's pickup needs to be selected or unidirectional.

However all moving coil, condenser and electret microphones can be designed to be unidirectional. The correct term for this pickup pattern or polar diagram, is cardioid and can be seen below.

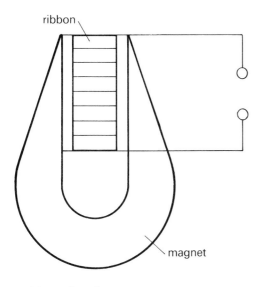

The ribbon microphone

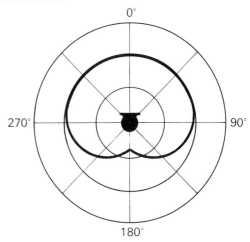

Cardioid polar diagram, most sensitive at 0°, less so at 90° and 270° and the least at 180° degrees.

This shows that the mic is very sensitive at the front and progressively less so at the sides and rear. Often mics are more directional than this in which case they are known as 'supercardioid' and more progessively 'hypercardioid', colloquially 'shotgun', 'rifle', or 'gun' mics. It is worth noting that a hypercardioid mic need not have the extended cylinder often associated with a rifle barrel but in fact it could resemble an ordinary hand-held cardioid. The hypercardioid mics' polar diagram is shown opposite.

All the previous polar diagrams have shown very basic curves. In fact, the pickup pattern is different for each frequency band, the mics being more directional to higher frequencies. So a diagram produced by the manufacturer might look like the one featured below.

Manufacturers polar diagrams showing variations with frequency, the diagrams also show the frequency response of the mic (AKG C414).

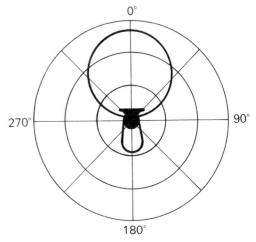

Hypercardioid polar diagram; sensitive only at 0°.

Frequency Response: Polar Diagrams:

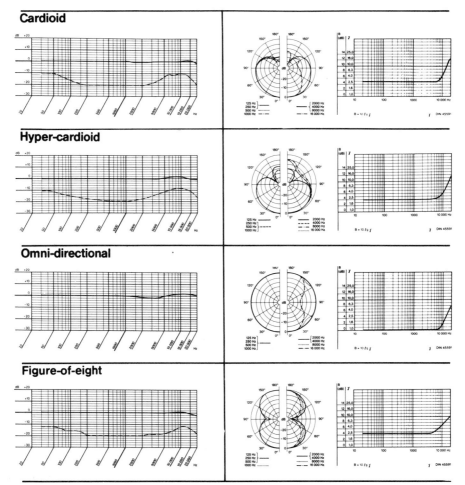

The response and performance of a microphone on its axis (in front at the 0 degree point) are obviously important, but so are they off axis (90 and 270 degrees to the side). It is here that the microphone hears the sound from loudspeakers and other performers and an awkward sensitivity pattern off-axis can produce many problems, especially howlround.

With all but the best cardioids, frequencies above 1kHz will deteriorate off axis (at 90 degrees to the mic) and although voice quality does not suffer too much, musical instruments with harmonics above 5kHz will not sound very bright, therefore the choice and positioning of mics for music is critical. The microphones' frequency response variation off axis is known as colouration, and one might talk of a mic not introducing too much colouration, that is emphasising or de-emphasising specific frequencies.

We will see later that the cardioid principle has also been applied to create a new form of microphone, the pressure zone mic where the pickup capsule is aimed at a small built-in plate, these are useful for discrete reinforcement along the footlights or in scenery. Finally stereo mics (more commonly associated with the recording studio) are also occasionally used. These mics comprise a pair of cardioid capsules aiming left and right and are used with appropriately positioned loudspeakers to generate an authentically reinforced sound, but we will see later that there are other methods of producing stereo sound reinforcement.

Yet another variation on the cardioid is the 'Differoid', this is actually a trade name (used by Crown International) but it is a compilation of the words 'cardioid' and 'differential'. This mic possesses standard cardioid properties when used close to the mouth but when the performer pulls back from the mic the level heard by the mic drops off much faster than with standard cardioids and the manufacturers indicate that once the performer is more than 3–4" away then the fall off can be as much as 25dB. Hence this mic provides excellent gain before feedback and could be especially useful in high sound level situations as a vocal mic.

QUALITY, RESPONSE AND SENSITIVITY

One of the last aspects of the microphone to be considered is its sensitivity. How much sound can it pick up? This is often called the output level. All measurements are compared to a reference level and since the amount of signal that the microphone provides is smaller than the reference level, the figure is expressed as a negative. Thus, where the reference level is 1 volt, we read of -50dB and -60dB, the nearer the number is to zero the more sensitive the mic (so in this case the -50dB mic would be the more sensitive of the two).

There is an alternative method of expressing sensitivity, which is based on the fact that a normal voice at a distance of 12" from the mic produces sound pressure of 1 dyne per cm^2. This corresponds to air pressure of 1 in microbars. This may now be used as the reference level, so that a high figure is given for a very sensitive microphone – say 5 millivolts per microbar or 5mv/μB, and a low figure for a less sensitive mic such as 0.2 millivolts per microbar or 0.2mv/μB. All such measurements are meaningless, unless the appropriate reference level is appreciated.

In terms of tonal quality it is desirable that the control is solely in the hands of the operator at the mixing desk, the mic itself should not introduce some emphasis or de-emphasis of frequencies on its own. In other words the response from the mic should be flat. Generally, condenser mics alone will provide completely flat responses. A good quality dynamic mic will have a response from 40Hz–16Hz without serious deviation, whereas the condenser frequently is flat 20Hz–20Hz. Dynamic mics often provide some boost to upper frequencies but this may not be undesirable since in vocals the slight mid or HF boost may help clarity because the consonants lie in the upper frequencies. Some people also like this 'presence' on musical instruments like the violin or harp.

RADIO MICROPHONES

There is often a need for a performer or musician to move freely about the stage and to be provided with a mic, but without the hindrance of the trailing cable. Radio mics, introduced into the theatre in the 1960s, are the answer but they are complex items and require knowledgeable attention for the best results.

There are two basic types, one a handheld mic which contains its own transmitter, and the other a concealed mic which works to a pocketsize transmitter also concealed on the performer. The latter is used in costume productions, musicals and pantomimes.

Handheld radio microphone with diversity receiver unit.

Each transmitter has its own receiver which then feeds the signal into the mixer input channel in the normal way. Transmitters require a power supply, either from batteries, which should be checked before every show if not changed, or from a built-in power supply which is recharged after each show, and transmitters have LEDs which warn when the battery life is low.

In the U.K. radio mics are approved by the Department of Trade and Industry to work over 27 frequencies (22 of them new). The mics must work within set limits and a large number of mics which are all on at once might effect a reduction in quality. Early radio mics had a tendency to 'drift' away from their allotted frequency and could also pick up other 'radio' traffic nearby – taxis being notorious. This can still happen occasionally and in the latter case it may be that some associated cabling – perhaps the earth wire – is the correct length to act as an aerial. Temporary installations are particularly prone to trouble having a tendency to loose wires and bad connections.

Today's radio mics do help to overcome some of these problems by being provided with meters and LEDs to warn of faults, but they still cannot

be checked enough and ideally a spare transmitter should be kept backstage for each mic in use. More expensive systems operate on the diversity principle whereby the system hunts across several aerial positions in the auditorium for the best response and 'locks' on the one offering the strongest reception.

In the case of concealed mics, either suspended round the neck or clipped to clothing, three things are vital:

1) The material must not generate static electricity – this tends to rule out silk garments. Clothes with metal supports can also cause problems.

2) The aerial lead must be straight and firm – not allowed to bend and break, it is best taped to the skin.

3) The mic itself should be as near the mouth as possible – unless specified otherwise most neck mics are omnidirectional and will generate feedback if the gain is really turned up – which it might need to be if the mic is buried at chest level. Small cardioid pickup capsules are available but they can lose some frequency response which might need correcting at the mixer. Since these mics are tiny they can also be concealed in wigs, and in all locations need frequent cleaning to remove perspiration and make-up.

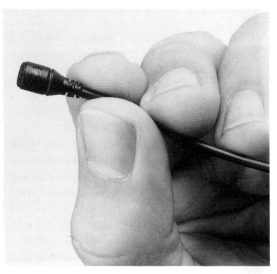

Small microphone associated with radio microphone transmitters and usually concealed in clothing or wigs, both omni and cardioid capsules are available, the one shown here is an electret mic.

Mics with switches should never be purchased – control should always be with the operator – but in radio mics sometimes a switch is an asset since offstage and dressing rooms conversation will be picked up by a neck mic which the performer cannot easily unplug and which the operator may have forgotten to fade out, of course he has to remember to switch it on again! Wherever radio mics are used it is vital that the mixing desk is fitted with a pre-fade-listen push so that the operator can listen in to the channel before the performer goes on stage and check that all is well.

SUMMARY

In theatre work the sound source is picked up by means of directional (cardioid or hypercardioid) mics. The frequency response of the mic should be as flat as possible, and with the output or sensitivity as high as possible, measured in decibels where a low figure is good, or in millivolts where a high figure is good. The mic's pickup-pattern at the side (off-axis) should not induce distortion, dullness or howlround. Generally there are two types of mics, dynamics which are sturdy, and condensers (and electrets) which are more sensitive and can have a flatter response. Condenser mics require a power supply which can either be inbuilt or supplied down the line (phantom powering).

Now we will pass to the next link in the chain, the sound mixer.

THE MIXER

It is at this point in the system that the inputs from the different sources are brought together, it is here that the volume of each input is controlled – and the point at which the tonal quality of each input can be adjusted, after which all the inputs can be combined into groups before the signals are sent to the amplifier.

Simple mixers usually have inputs set for specific purposes – mic, tape, disc etc., and they rarely have many facilities (quite often just one overall tone control rather than one per channel). Consequently they are more suited to public address

A selection of mixers with inbuilt power amplifiers ideal for small systems and public address.

than to theatre, and quite often for this function this type of mixer is provided with a built-in amplifier.

Theatre or recording mixing desks have input channels which can accept both mics and recording equipment (to a defined level known as 'line level' which is the standard output level of professional equipment) and each channel will be fitted with tone controls.

A large modular theatre mixer, this one provides 32 inputs and 8 main outputs.

Both kinds of mixers can be found with controls mounted on a single fascia plate, or where each input section is on a separate frame (module) so that it plugs in and out – these are known as modular mixers and, whilst being more

A mixer input module being removed from the desk, such mixers are easy to maintain and expand.

expensive, are the more desirable since mainten-ance and expansion are easier.

Now let us look at some of the facilities that are required of a good theatre mixer.

INPUT/MIC/LINE/SUBMIXING

The more simple mixers which tend to have inputs designated for specific uses (tape, disc etc) are restrictive in multi-purpose work – one show might use a lot of mics – the other a lot of effects and perhaps the mixer cannot adapt to cope with both uses. A good mixer has two inputs per channel that are selectable – one at mic level, the other at line level and the selection is usually made by a switch on the input module. Thus a 16 input desk could accept 16 mics or 16 inputs at line level (for tape decks etc) or any combination of the two.

Line level inputs also accept the output from other (often hired) mixers which might be brought in (to serve the orchestra mix or extra mics needed during the annual pantomime or large musicals), this process is known as sub-mixing. It is quite useful if the mixers serve clear sections of the overall mix so that the main system would master all mixers and handle vocals leaving the submixers to handle orchestra, foldback or effects. Quite often in these situa-tions the subs are not positioned with the main mixer but with the musicians.

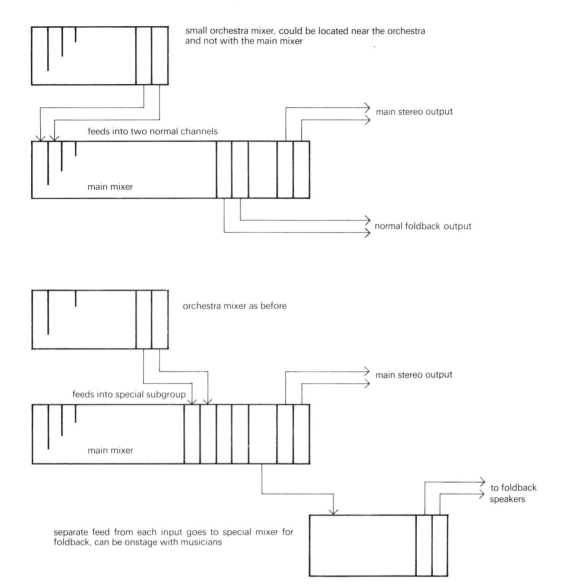

small orchestra mixer, could be located near the orchestra and not with the main mixer

main stereo output

feeds into two normal channels

main mixer

normal foldback output

orchestra mixer as before

main stereo output

feeds into special subgroup

main mixer

to foldback speakers

separate feed from each input goes to special mixer for foldback, can be onstage with musicians

Submixers and their relationship to the main mixer.

GAIN/SENSITIVITY/VOLUME

If a singer or an instrument is producing too much level then the mic could feed a larger signal than is desirable to the later parts of the chain which might be thus overloaded. In these situations it is necessary to control this sound before it reaches the main part of the mixer channel. This is done by providing a sensitivity or coarse gain control (like a volume control) actually on the input to the mixer. The sensitivity control affects both mic and line levels (though less so in the latter case since the range of power is smaller). We will see later that a system must be able to cope with some extra level (offering 'headroom') and how this might be calculated.

The output of the channel is provided with a volume control usually in the form of a linear-motion fader calibrated in points or decibels. The two controls are set so that maximum gain at the

LINE LEVEL INPUT JACK
$\frac{1}{4}$" Jack accepts balanced or
unbalanced signals.

MICROPHONE INPUT XLR
Electronically balanced input
with phantom powering.

PHANTOM POWER SWITCH
On/off switch for microphone
powering

INSERT JACK
Pre-equaliser insertion point.

INPUT GAIN
Adjusts pre-amplifier to suit
various input levels.

PAD SWITCH
Reduces Mic input by 18 dB or
line input by 12 dB.

HF CONTROL
Shelving characteristic with $\pm$ 12
dB cut/boost at a corner frequency of 8 kHz.

HIGH MF CONTROL
Peaking characteristic with $\pm$ 12
dB cut/boost at a centre frequency of 3.5 Hz.

LOW MF CONTROL
Peaking characteristic with $\pm$ 12
dB cut/boost at a centre frequency of 250 Hz.

LF CONTROL
Shelving characteristic with $\pm$ 12
dB cut/boost at a corner frequency of 80 Hz.

EQ CUT SWITCH
Bypass switch for the equaliser
section allowing instant
comparison.

AUX SEND LEVELS A, B, C, D
Allows up to four mixes of input sources for
foldback, echo and cue mixes. A & B post
fade, C & D pre eq, (internal links allow
optional pre eq, pre fade or post fade sends.)

ASSIGNMENT SWITCHES
Selects the channel to groups 1 -
4 or L - R outputs.

PAN CONTROL
Used to position the input in the
stereo field or between a pair of groups.

PFL SWITCH
Monitors pre fader signal to allow
cueing of input signal.

MUTE SWITCH
Cuts all post fader signal sends.

PEAK INDICATOR
LED warns of imminent overload (clipping).

CHANNEL FADER
100 mm Alps fader with 10 dB
boost available.

INPUT CHANNEL
M110

GROUP OUTPUT XLR
Electronically balanced output.

TAPE INPUT JACK (5 - 8)
Dual level input connector.

TAPE INPUT JACK (1 - 4)
Dual level input connector.

GROUP INSERT JACK
Pre-fader insertion point.

GROUP METER
10 segment VU characteristic
display giving visual indication of
group output signal level.

**TAPE (5 - 8) RETURN
SECTION**
Aux send (D), level and pan
controls feeding stereo output.
Input signals can be selected
between group output or tape
input for monitoring during
recording but can also be used as
additional Fx returns during
sound reinforcement.

**TAPE (1 - 4) RETURN
SECTION**
As Tape (5 - 8) above.

GROUP PFL SWITCH
Monitors pre fader signal to allow
cueing of group signals.

PEAK INDICATOR
LED warns of imminent overload
(clipping).

GROUP FADER
100 mm Alps fader with 10 dB
boost available.

GROUP OUTPUT
M120

A selection of modules from the Allen and Heath SRC range.

output fader does not produce feedback in normal circumstances and also allows the output fader to be able to use all its travel for smoother fades. Generally the output fader is positioned so that some extra gain is always in hand for emergencies.

Closely positioned to the input gain control a good mixer also offers a Phase invert switch which reverses the polarity of the connections so that microphones are all in phase and their signals do not cancel each other out, this is desirable if people bring their own mics which might be wired differently to those owned by the theatre itself.

TONE CONTROL/EQUALISATION

Each channel is listening to a different source and therefore should have the facility to make tonal corrections to that source without affecting any others. At the very least each input channel should be provided with a separate bass and treble control and adjustment to boost or cut amounts of each. As a rule on vocal mics the treble will be boosted if clarity is needed; the bass cut a little to prevent feedback. Feedback can of course occur at any frequency although it is more likely to occur at the more omni-directional lower frequencies.

On simple mixers the frequency at which both tone controls operate will be fixed, usually at 100Hz for the bass and 10kHz for the treble. A good mixer should provide a boost or cut, shown as plus/minus of at least 12dB, 16dB being common. However, both these frequencies are outside the range of most human fundamental frequencies so tonal adjustment on vocals is affecting the harmonics only. The provision of a middle or presence control greatly helps because this affects the main part of the vocal spectrum. Sometimes this control is set at a specific frequency – or there may be several individual controls to handle the whole middle band where all the frequencies are selectable. Again adjustment of plus/minus at least 12dB is desirable (but some mixers only allow for a boost at this point).

Sophisticated mixers provide extra controls still so that three or four out of fifteen or more frequencies may be selected right across the spectrum. This is certainly useful – especially where musical instruments are involved. In such a case, it is desirable to be able to effect momentary comparisons with the original uncorrected sound and since tonal work is known as equalisation, the appropriate button is called the EQ cut.

After being equalised the input signal is then routed to the various ancilliary outputs before passing to the main output fader.

AUXILIARIES/ECHO/FOLDBACK

Singers and musicians need to hear their contribution clearly over the main sound to judge the quality of their performance. The best way to achieve this is to provide them with a system separate from the main system and which works from this routing section of the mixer. This system is known as foldback. There may be several systems each feeding vocalists, percussion, lead guitar and strings, each wanting to hear part of their own sound plus others. A recent development has been the radio transmission of these chains of foldback to each musician who is provided with a receiver and a small mixer where he can blend the kind of foldback he alone desires before sending it on to his headset or small adjacent loudspeaker. On some concerts the foldback system is more complex (and louder!) than the main sound system and is often controlled by the musicians themselves from their own sub-mixer on stage.

Echo is desirable on a vocal mic to give it some depth – though it is rarely a separate echo – more of a reverberation (a prolonging of the last syllable) and it is provided not within the mixer but from an external device that then feeds the sound back to the main group outputs again. The echo and foldback controls are known as auxiliaries, and can either be set before (pre) the channel fader so that the effect is governed by and varies with the channel fader or after (post) the channel fader so that the level of the effect is governed solely by the auxiliary control itself.

PREFADE LISTEN – OVERLOAD – INSERT

This valuable little facility, ideally a momentary action push, allows the operator to listen to the channel signal without it passing into the audience. It is used to check that offstage mics and radio mics are working and also to line up tapes and other recordings.

Good mixers provide an insert point on each channel in order to add extra facilities from an external piece of equipment (plugged in at the rear), typical cases are perhaps more equalisation on a main vocal channel, or some noise reduction in the case of a tape channel. Rock musicians also insert noise gates (of which more later) to sharpen the system's attack time and provide crisper sound. Ideally the insert facility should allow the external device to be switched in or out of the system from the desk itself.

The overload light is an indicator of when the channel's overload point has been reached (this is determined by the manufacturer). It enables the operator to determine which is the danger channel by eye, rather than by listening which is sometimes not easy in a complex mix.

Finally in this section some mixers provide a Channel on switch which is useful in conference work where a delegate mic might be set at a predetermined level and switched on and off at will.

GROUP ROUTING

These controls combine different inputs together and send the signals to the main output groups. Usually the choice of groups reflect some aspect of the show each of which requires a master fader all to itself – vocal mics, orchestra mics, general mics, radios, tapes etc. An alternative could be – vocals left, vocals right, orchestra left, orchestra right, in which case the controls would switch in a stereo balance control known as

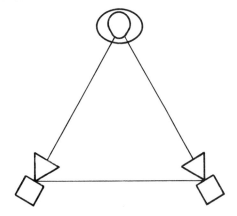

Perfect stereo image is created by the listener and speakers being an equal distance from each other.

PAN. This sends the single sound source to two or more pairs of output groups and offers a variation on the percentage going to one side or the other, generally the pair of outputs are associated with left and right loudspeaker groups. Of course since the correct reproduction of stereo sound is only possible if the listener is the same distance from the speakers as they are from each other, in a traditional proscenium theatre for some people one loudspeaker could predominate over the other, thus correct theatre stereo can only be limited to people in the centre stalls.

Hence stereo in theatre terms suggests a broadening of the aural canvas, which would be desirable for stage band set-ups which often use loudspeakers at each side of the stage, mixing the sound of the instruments so that they favour the nearest loudspeaker so that the visual and aural pictures match. If no separate vocal loudspeaker systems are provided (such as a cluster hung over the proscenium) vocal mics would be routed to both groups. Float pickup and rifle pickup mics are also often routed to favour their appropriate side; note that the routing should not be extreme, just a slight emphasis on one side or another.

(A variation on this technique, called Deltastereophony, delays the loudspeaker output relative to the mic's distance from the source giving emphasis to the loudspeaker nearest to the source of the sound.)

The pan control does allow for a sound effect – recorded in mono – to be 'panned', that is moved, from one side of the theatre to the other as the effect is played. This is obviously useful for effects in which transportation is featured. A similar effect is achievable with the 'quad pot', a joystick with four (or more) corners selectable in different amounts at random. These four could represent the four corners of the theatre so that with appropriately positioned loudspeakers an effect might appear to move behind the audience.

The pan control can also be a simple two-grouping selector in the extreme left or right position (with outputs not necessarily being routed to left and right, but perhaps stalls/circle or stage effects/stalls effects).

In all cases effects should never be so spectacular as to distract the audience from the play.

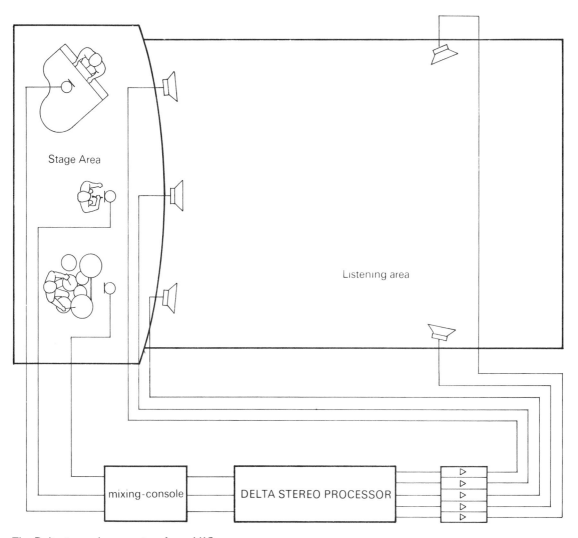

The Deltastereophony system from AKG.

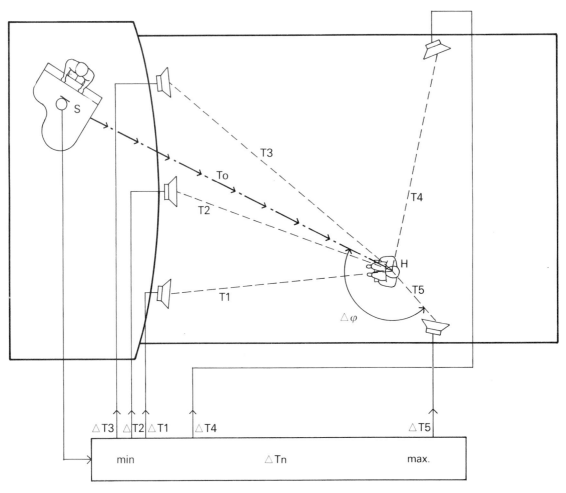

Acoustical Principle of the Delta Stereophony System

$\Delta\varphi$ ... *Angle between visual and acoustic stimulus (without delay devices)*

To ... *Acoustic delay of direct sound waves (unamplified)*

Tn ... *Acoustic delays* (T1, T2, T3, ...)

ΔTn ... *Electrical delay times* (ΔT1, ΔT2, ΔT3, ...)

S ... *Sound source*

H ... *Listener location*

ΔTn To-Tn

OUTPUT GROUPS – SUBGROUPS

As we have seen above it is possible to route the input signals to any output group or combination of output groups – relating to the orchestra, general pickup, vocals and so on. Mixers are normally provided with at least two outputs, with most professional systems offering at least four and frequently eight. A larger number provides for greater flexibility.

Each output group is provided with a fader and usually an echo-return volume control. Some mixers provide small equalisers with eight (octave) filters, these need careful use since tone control is also possible on the input module and later in the system by the main graphic equaliser which compensates for the theatre's acoustics. However, sometimes it is desirable to make over-

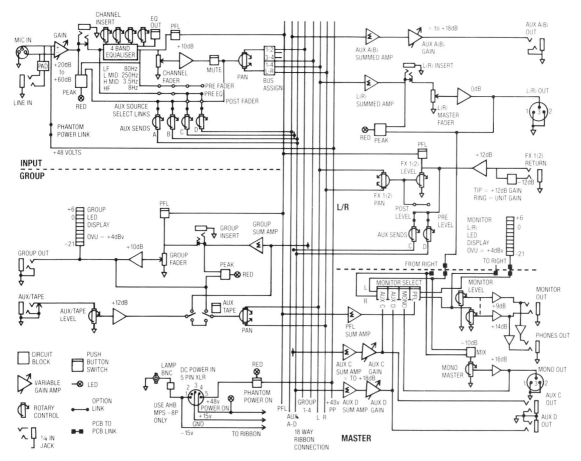

Block schematic of the Allen and Heath SR mixer

all corrections to a group. There is no standard set of accepted facilities that should be available at this point; prefade listen, stereo pan and foldback are sometimes found.

Sometimes the groups are actually subdivisions of two main outputs, in which case they are called 'subgroups' handling a 'submix'. If an external submixer was used, its output would normally be fed into the system at this point rather than into an ordinary input channel which would be a waste, although technically quite possible on line level equipment.

Vu AND PPM METERS

Although the operator should be positioned so that he can hear the same sound that the audience hears it is necessary for him to be able to reasonably predict what an adjustment in a fader will mean in terms of output level. Good mixers therefore possess meters at the output stages which relate the loudness to a scale. In fact the

scale indicates apparent loudness but is actually based on a measurement of the amount of electrical current flowing through the mixer output.

All meters are provided with a reference point on their scale and the individual input channels should be set up with their gain or sensitivity and main fader so that a particular movement of each fader produces a known response relevant to the reference point on the scale of the output meter. A good mixer will provide a tone that can be fed into the system to assist in the correct adjustment relative to the original reference point and a good sound engineer will put a reference tone on a sound effects tape for the same reason.

Meters operate according to two different ballistics, Vu (Volume unit) or PPM (Peak Programme Meter), and some meters can be switched from one to the other. Both types of meter may provide their information either on a conventional scale, or by means of coloured light-emitting diodes, LEDs. The latter are easier to assimilate in the theatre's usual darkness, especially since they change colour at specific points in the scale. Bargraph, plasma and video displays are also available.

The output of a theatre mixer showing LED meters; these are easy to read in the theatre's usual darkness and change colour at various levels.

Vu meters in the output section of a theatre mixer.

The more common meter, Vu, is cheaper than the PPM and the quicker acting – so it can be difficult to read. It has two scales – one which represents percentage use of the channel (its measurements are often arbitrary), the other representing a decibel scale. On the Vu meter 'O' represents a reading of +4dB above zero level (1mw into 600 ohms), and most of the travel will be between −3 and +3.

Broadcast and recording authorities prefer the slower PPM which is more precise and easier to read in potential overload situations. It has a seven point scale – each point representing 4dB. On the PPM meter the line up is usually on 4 so that a reading of 6 would suggest overload being 8dB over line up (although occasional peaks are usually acceptable).

The final analysis of course is that the operator must watch the show and use his ears (assuming of course that the operator is well placed to hear the show!) rather than dumbly adhere to a meter setting; the meter is a guide rather than the final arbiter. In recording, the meter would have more precedence which indicates the importance of the reference line-up levels.

MONITORING/LISTENING TO THE SHOW

There has been a tendency in the past to position the mixer in a hermetically sealed control room where the operator is forced to rely on loudspeakers for monitoring the level and quality of the show itself. One mistake often made in this situation is to spend more money on control room monitors than on main speakers. The two should match, otherwise the operator cannot have an accurate idea of what his tonal corrections are doing to the frequency response of the main speakers. There are occasions (such as pre-listening and lining up tapes) when the operator requires either a headset or monitor loudspeaker but otherwise he must be positioned so as to accurately perceive the level and quality as perceived by the audience – and to satisfy this concern he must be in the same acoustic as the audience.

In recording the monitors should be of the highest quality so that all the content can be heard without any colouration or exclusion by the speakers themselves, although once the recording has been approved it is wise to play it over the loudspeakers which will serve the audience.

Popular small powered monitor loudspeaker ideal for control areas both for the main programme and communications.

Most new control positions are now being located in the stalls or circle in a small pen – or in a control room with most of the viewing wall removable. Despite this improvement the operator must still be aware of a number of factors which govern his perception of the sound level. First the rear stall control position will almost inevitably have a circle overhang which is likely to prevent much of the main loudspeaker beam from directly reaching the operator, causing a 'sound shadow'. Secondly in all but the best systems the sound level is usually higher closer to the loudspeakers and so the operator must be aware that an acceptable sound level for him might be uncomfortable for the audience nearer to the loudspeakers at say the front and side stalls. Finally he should be aware that the ambient sound level is higher in the middle of the main auditorium than it is at the rear, this is especially true in productions aimed at children, and so the operator will need to compensate. Finally of course the operator must be on the centre line of the loudspeakers if he is mixing stereo.

CHOOSING THE MIXER – THE SPECIFICATION

Adhering to the chain theorem it is not possible to have one link more important than another, but certainly the mixer link requires careful thought. Mixers are very attractive items, almost the only part of the sound system not confining its secrets to a satin anodised box, but bringing them out onto the surface with knobs to twiddle and dials to watch. Care is taken over their shape and appearance, their colour and weight. Mixers are sexy and consequently it is easy to make the wrong choice; the cosmetic can appeal over the economic and the practical.

Try to choose a mixer that is modular – this will make maintenance, flexibility and expansion easier than those mixers with controls mounted on a single fascia. Next, choose a mixer big enough for your needs – then add some. Sound mixes have grown incredibly and don't show any signs of levelling out. The number of input channels and output channels should be carefully considered and, if possible, the overall frame big enough to make additions later by taking out a blank module and inserting the new channel.

Consider where the unit is to be used – are the doors wide enough for the desk to be brought in? – an often overlooked fact. What is the lighting like and what colour is it? Can the dials and calibrations be easily seen in such dim (and often coloured) light?

If your sound engineer leaves and the next one works in a different way, will the system be flexible enough to cope with the change – or is it so specialised that only he can understand it? Does the manufacturer offer training programmes?

These are some of the general questions. The question of the mixer's performance is also important, and one of the most telling aspects is the signal to noise ratio.

SIGNAL TO NOISE RATIO

Noise is defined as the random movements of electrons within a system, and it can be detected as a hissing or rushing water sound. It is important that this noise does not rise to a disturbing level as the gain of the mixer is turned up and theatre mixers usually work at very high sound levels. A s/n ratio of 70dB would be acceptable for good quality voice reinforcement, but the standard to aim for would be 95–100dB, suitable for a system delivering very high sounds. (This would exclude most 'public address' type systems from theatre work.) It should be remembered that a sound system is installed for a long time and the premise that 'we don't have high sound levels here' is not acceptable since it ignores future possibilities.

Each item in a sound system should have as flat a response as possible over the range 20Hz to 20,000Hz, even if the system's loudspeakers have a narrower response. This is to avoid reproducing damaging harmonics that might arise from a problem fundamental which is itself below the range of the loudspeaker and otherwise ignored.

The manufacturer should also be asked about driving the system hard, how much overload, how much headroom is there in the mixer – how much punishment can it take. Some manufacturers quote figures for the degree of sound the system will stand with reference to an agreed overload point.

Summary

The mixer is the device which receives all the inputs to the sound system and provides them with a means of being balanced and combined before they pass to the amplifier. The input signals may also be adjusted with respect to their tonal content. A modular mixer enables maintenance to be easily carried out; it also allows for future expansion. Other mixers may be connected to the main mixer to expand the system, this is known as sub-mixing and is especially suited to orchestral mics. The mixer may have several outputs, some of which are for auxiliary purposes such as echo (via an external device) or foldback (so that the artist and orchestra may hear themselves).

The equaliser and filters

By the nature of its shape and furnishing the auditorium can alter and colour the sound coming from the loudspeakers. This is usually undesirable since some frequencies can be accentuated and it is at these points that feedback or howlround will occur first. Even without this possibility it is obviously pointless to go to the expense of providing a good system only to have some external element, such as the building, take over and effect its own control.

Corrections to the overall sound can be made by filters. The most common being the shelving filter, where the amount of change ceases after a pre-determined level (this kind is usually found on mixers) or the bandpass filter, where the response curves towards and away from the selected frequency (this is the type of filter usually employed in graphic equalisers). A parametric filter or equaliser is one that may change the frequency or rate of attentuation of the alteration. Generally speaking, the bass and treble controls on mixers are set at specific frequencies but the mid or presence control may be adjustable over a range of frequencies and so said to be 'parametric'. Extremely fine adjustments can be made by a 'notch filter' which is set to affect only a very small part of the audio spectrum, these are useful where there is interference from outside devices or where the auditorium creates an unusual 'spike' in the acoustic.

The graphic equaliser is the most common way to correct the harmful influences of the auditorium. It is inserted into the chain between mixer and power amplifier and it splits up the audio band into a number of filters each of which

A parametric equaliser.

15 band graphic equalisers, the top for use where space is at a premium.

may be boosted or cut by at least 12dB, ideally 16dB. The equalisers are usually lined up for a particular acoustic or type of production, and then not adjusted till either the production or the acoustic is changed, they should not be adjusted at whim although many models offer a memory of the settings and allow several different settings to be recorded. This is especially useful in multi-purpose auditoria where there may be several physical changes or where sound systems are toured, the group being able to tune virtually any auditorium to their standard acoustic.

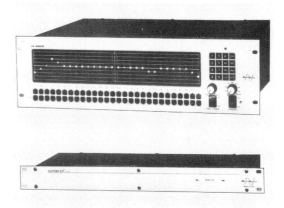

Combined analyser and equaliser showing the house curve on the LED display, this unit offers eight room settings which can be reproduced from the device's memory.

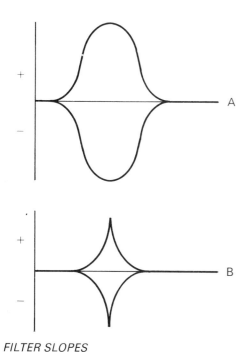

FILTER SLOPES
A shows the gentle bandpass filter found in graphic equalisers, B shows the sharper notch filter used to corrrect specific problem frequencies.

Some graphic equalisers are little more than sophisticated tone controls because they operate at octave centres and provide only for 11 filters, and because the upper octaves are well separated there may be a troublesome frequency in between the filter points. Professional equalisers therefore set the filters at one-third octave centres. Sometimes it is preferable to adjust filters on either side of a problem frequency, even though there may actually be a filter for that frequency. That is because the whole nature of the sound is changed this way, and often the reduction in overall level is less than if a finer correction had been made.

The adjustment of graphic equalisers is complex and in the hand of the uninitiated the device can create more problems than it solves. Some people claim that the equaliser can be set by ear alone but the provision of a device known as a spectrum analyser greatly eases the task. Equal amounts of all frequencies (called pink noise, white noise is equal amounts per octave) are fed into the speaker system and picked up by microphones placed on stage and in the auditorium. The analyser then provides a read-out of just how the system and the acoustics have altered the original input, this is known as the 'house curve'. The graphic equaliser is then adjusted relative to the read-out so that peaks and troughs are evened out. The analyser operates in 'real-time' so that its display adjusts as the equaliser is being adjusted and a good model also offers a memory display of the equalised and unequalised sound. Some designers (the author included) bias the monitoring microphones to stage positions so that the equalised system takes more account of likely feedback points and provides more gain. (There is also evidence that systems equalised on the loudspeakers' axis produce damaging responses off axis.)

An alternative room correction system (called SIM) compares the output from the mixer directly with the output of the loudspeakers and offers phasing adjustments as well as equalisation. Since this system works with any output from the mixer (rather than with pink noise) the system can be used during performances affecting constant improvement.

Equalisers can be inserted at any point in the audio chain before the amplifier – they may be connected to a specific piece of equipment, and in complex systems favoured by rock groups, may be found on each item, but generally they are found after the outputs from the mixer. Ideally they should be connected to each part of the system that is separately fed – so that stalls left and right loudspeakers (in a stereo set-up) would need two – one in a mono set-up. If the theatre had other tiers, this pattern would be repeated. The equaliser could also be used on a foldback system – the artist's own stage monitor speaker – but if there is a troublesome frequency that causes feedback mid-way between even the tight bands of the one third octave system then the answer is to provide a 'notch' filter which effects a sharp attentuation at the selected point.

Many people feel that equalisers are a luxury – this is very foolish thinking. Not only do they afford a real chance of cutting down feedback, but also of adjusting the quality of the sound.

SUMMARY

The graphic equaliser is a collection of individual filters which may be adjusted to improve the quality and gain of the overall sound. The device usually corrects peaks or troughs in the 'house curve' – the response of a particular acoustic to a particular system.

THE AMPLIFIER

Up to now, on its journey from mic or tape, through mixer and equaliser, the sound signal has lacked strength. The amplifier is the next item in the chain and the one which provides the signal with the strength to drive the loudspeakers.

Amplifiers need to be carefully selected because their performance can be adversely affected by a number of factors, mainly distortion, overload or short circuit (caused by some fault in the wiring external to the amp). However professional amplifiers have much improved over recent years and all have protection against these factors quite often resulting in an automatic cut-out if danger threatens.

Amplifiers are prone to noise, which as we saw in the mixer was the random movement of electrons in the system. Distortion must obviously be kept to a minimum, since the signal must not leave the amp altered in style. Harmonic distortion is possibly the most disturbing, usually affecting the odd numbered harmonics in a way which can produce discordant results unnatural to the ear. Occasionally the amplifier will affect only part of the audio band – perhaps cutting down the bass and making the result 'tinny'.

Another kind of distortion is called amplitude distortion – or 'clipping'. This occurs when the unit simply cannot handle the amount of signal being fed to the input and in the past this problem was the most likely since it lay outside the control of the amp itself. Today amplifiers are fitted with a variety of processor-based circuitry which is programmed to sense clipping and automatically proportionately reduce the overload, this 'limiting' function protects the loudspeakers without affecting the overall performance of the system. Processor controlled amplifiers also offer read-outs (via compatible PCs) of average and peak power and also of temperature.

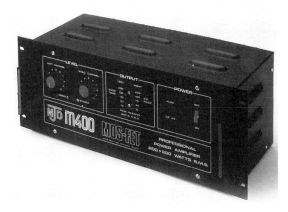

200 watt stereo power amplifer showing fault, temperature and peak readouts on the fascia.

Typical performance figures for a good amplifier would be for total harmonic distortion (referred to usually as THD): less than 0.01% at rated output at a frequency of 1kHz. Two important points here are that the figure should relate to a quoted frequency and to a quoted power output. A distortion figure of above 0.1% would not be desirable in high quality systems. The specification would also quote the frequency response which should be as flat as possible within 20Hz–20kHz, (a deviation of +3dB would be acceptable over this range) and the specification should again indicate at what impedance this was measured. Finally there would also be the noise figure which should be quoted against the rated output – a figure of over 100dB is desirable.

RMS OR PEAK –
POWER AND WATTS

Amplifiers deliver their output in two ways, low impedance and constant voltage, and terms associated with the output are 'rms' – root mean square – and 'peak'. 'Peak', as its name suggests, refers to occasional momentary high points and is also sometimes referred to as 'music' power. RMS is the average output of the system and the figure normally quoted since it is important to ascertain what the amplifier can deliver for long periods rather than for moments ('peak' is usually double the rms value).

A professional power amplifier will express different powers into different loads, such as 340w rms into 4 ohm, 210w rms into 8 ohms, and 110w rms into 16 ohms. It would be usual to utilise the 8 ohm figure, especially if just one loudspeaker was being connected. However some designers of large systems favour the 4 ohm output since it provides more power.

Remembering the two basic electrical equations:

$$Watts = volts \times amps$$
$$volts = amps \times ohms$$

we can produce a third:

$$volts^2 = ohms \times watts$$

We can therefore see that a system delivering 100w rms to an 8 ohm loudspeaker does so at just over 28 volts, about $3\frac{1}{2}$ amps. If two 8 ohm speakers were connected in a series to form a 16 ohm load then there would not be sufficient voltage to drive them, and there would be a consequent loss of power. Conversely, if two 8 ohm units were connected in parallel, forming a 4 ohm load, there would be too much voltage, and distortion would result.

When matching amplifiers to loudspeakers it is important that the amplifier can deliver the power needed to reach the peaks above the rms or normal programme level. This extra capacity is known as headroom and we shall see later how it can be calculated but generally it means that no amplifier should be used at more than half or two thirds of its rated value. Amplifier gain is usually expressed in watts as a measure of the power available from the product of the voltage and the current but some specifications alternatively express the gain of the unit in decibels. This figure should state clearly what is being used as the reference point, and whether it is a comparison therefore of power or voltage.

For example suppose that 100w output was achieved from 0.1w input. This would be a ratio of 1000:1 or 10^3:1 which is 30dB of gain on power, and this would be the figure normally quoted. (This is also 60dB of gain on voltage since voltage increases 6dB for every 3dB increase in power.)

Most amplifiers have a preset gain control so that their outputs can be regulated accordingly and the best systems restrict one amplifier to each speaker, or speaker group in which case the preset gain becomes another fine local gain control relative to the geography of the theatre. In this format all amplifiers should have the same rating, which then makes it easy for one spare to be available for anywhere in the system. This technique prevents overload, allows precise balancing of one part of the theatre against another – and doesn't put all the system's eggs into one basket. Failure of one amp loses only part, not the whole, of the system.

Control area showing amplifiers, equalisers and associated equipment in tamper-proof racks with lockable doors.

Whenever one piece of sound equipment is switched on there is an inevitable surge of power down the line to the next piece of equipment. If the amplifiers are switched on before the mixer then the surge could damge the loudspeakers, hence the amplifiers are switched on last and switched off first. In large systems it is unwise to switch all the amplifiers on simultaneously and circuits can be arranged which power up each amplifier in turn (called soft start). For the same reason all faders on the mixer should be pulled down before any fault finding takes place (this particularly applies to checking for loose connections) or before tapes are rewound.

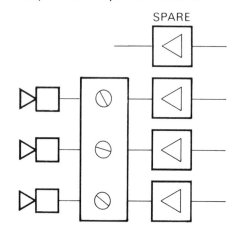

A panel of preset gain controls inserted to allow speakers to be balanced and those settings maintained when amps are changed.

100V LINE OR LOW IMPEDANCE

Low impedance refers to the kind of resistances offered to the circuit by the loudspeaker and it is measured in ohms (the usual professional loudspeaker is rated at 8 ohms). Constant voltage systems are used as an alternative where more than one speaker is required to be driven from one amplifier. Since transformers are involved there is some loss of frequency response and therefore these systems (called 100v line in U.K.; 70v line in U.S.) are usually restricted to paging and to public address. The limiting factor on a 100v line system is that the amp should not be overloaded. In the constant voltage system the power delivered from each loudspeaker is decided by its inbuilt transformer, and these often have several 'tappings' for different powers, or even a rotary volume control. This is useful since in a multispeaker set-up – fed from one amp – different locations may require different amounts of power, the main volume control dictating the overall balance. A 100w rms 100v amp could feed 100×1w rms speakers, or

10 × 10w speakers, or 1 × 100w speaker without problems – all other elements are matched by the transformers, and the cable length and type are relatively unimportant. Without the transformer – the low impedance system provides quality and is therefore the professional standard, but in the low impedance system the entire system external to the amp has to be matched – the length of cable and its size also offering resistance. Long runs from amp to speakers can be expensive, because the cable needs to be thick to offer little resistance. For this reason, low impedance amps are often kept as near as possible to the loudspeakers that they serve, otherwise some loss of power might occur down the line if the cable is not to be expensive. Constant voltage systems do not have this problem and therefore their amplifiers may be positioned anywhere; usually some remote control room or electrical switch room.

DISTRIBUTION AMPLIFIERS AND ATTENUATORS

As we have seen above, it is wise not to drive more than one loudspeaker from one amplifier and this suggests that a mixer output would therefore be feeding several amplifiers. The output of most professional mixers is sufficiently powerful to do this but where there are other items in the line, such as equalisers and crossovers, then the power reaching the amplifier could be reduced. In these cases distribution amplifiers are inserted to boost the signal. Each mixer output could have several distribution amplifiers each in turn providing several outputs and since each distribution amp is fitted with a gain control the device also permits further adjustments to the overall system balance.

Occasionally one device feeds too much signal to the next item in the chain and in order to prevent overloading an attenuator (sometimes called a pad) is fitted. The most useful type of these devices are built into the XLR connectors commonly used and so can easily be inserted into the circuit. Typical values are from 10dB to 60dB of attenuation in 10dB steps and the devices are available either at 200 ohm for mics or 600 ohm for line level equipment.

SUMMARY

The power amplifier accepts signals from the mixer and amplifies them sufficiently to drive the loudspeaker. Its output is measured in average terms – rms – and can either be matched to a constant voltage system (100v line) which is suitable to public address where several speakers are involved, or to a low impedance system (typically 8 ohm) where each amplifier would normally serve one speaker, in any event the amplifier should not be used at more than two-thirds of its rated output.

CHANGING THE SOUND – SIGNAL PROCESSING

Before we come to the loudspeaker, the last link in the chain, there are several other pieces of equipment which are used to control the sound in some way, and which may be inserted into the chain between the mixer and loudspeaker.

FREQUENCY SHIFTERS – FEEDBACK CORRECTION

Howlround, more commonly called feedback, will occur at a specific gain setting on any system, namely the point at which the system's output has been altered by the acoustic so that one particular frequency or frequency band is more prevalent (and therefore more likely to find its way back into the microphone). Some reduction in feedback can be effected by inserting graphic equalisers between the mixer and the amplifiers and tuning out prominent frequencies. It is also desirable to reduce bass response, and use directional mics and speakers, so that the sound is less likely to find its way back into the microphone.

Normally both input and output sound waves are in perfect sympathy – they are in phase; but a frequency shifter adjusts the output (rarely by more than by 5Hz) so that it is not in phase with the input and in a room that is fairly 'dead' – i.e. one with a low reverberation time – up to 6dB extra gain is possible before feedback re-occurs. The frequency shift however can disrupt the relation of live musical harmonics to those of amplified musical harmonics, and since this can be audible and disturbing, these devices should be restricted to vocal mics only and not used on instruments.

Another useful device is the phase inverter, which inverts the polarity of the voltage applied to the loudspeaker; this it does in pulses, keeping the escalation of feedback down. This device is credited with 4dB improvement in gain under normal conditions.

Generally speaking, these devices are extra items, added on to the main system although some mixers (notably those produced in the United States and Japan) have these devices built in.

LIMITERS AND COMPRESSORS

The job of the mixer and its operator is to balance the levels of the sound arriving at the input. Some levels may be very low and require lifting, others may be high and require holding down. Limiters and compressors help the operator to keep control over the extremes of the levels; compressors holding up the low levels and limiters keeping down the high levels. Some devices offer both functions.

For example, if a production has sources with a range of 60db then the lower levels might be swamped by the higher levels and so compression could be considered. In this case if the desired range is 30dB then a compression ratio of 2:1 is needed and this would raise the −60dB sounds by 30dB, the −40dB sounds by 20dB and the −20dB sounds by 10dB. However excessive compression can bring the background noise level dangerously high and threaten to mask some important information, a current feature of some location video and film sound in which actors who do not project find their voices masked by the compressed background 'atmosphere' sound.

A limiter leaves the sound unaltered until the levels reach maximum, at which point it would then reduce them to a determined level but the only part of the sound affected is that at the very peak – say within 3dB of maximum, a ratio of 20:1 over a range of 60dB.

The section of sound being controlled is called the threshold and the length of time the limiter holds the sound in its control can be selected before it is allowed to die away or decay.

Both of these devices find much work in the field of pop music where high levels are common and therefore the likelihood of overload is high and limiting is valuable to protect the loudspeaker. At the same time some compression is useful to lift quieter sounds so that they may compete more fairly. Both these devices are often applied to individual instruments or sections of the mixer as well as to the whole. Some mixers provide limiter/compressors in each input channel or subgroup channel.

NOISE GATE

The noise gate, allows sound to pass into the system once a predetermined sound level has been reached. This means that a mic would only be live when a direct sound, vocal or instrumental, is applied to it and therefore at other times it would not add extraneous noises to the mix. A higher system gain is often the result since the effective overall system gain decreases 3dB every time the number of mics in use doubles. These devices can also be set to switch in quickly or slowly, this is known as the 'attack' time, and to die away quickly or slowly, which is known as the 'decay' time. The shape of the resultant sound is the 'envelope'. These units are again found most often in pop music and can vastly shape the sound that we hear, for example a fast attack time on drums giving a very crisp sharp sound.

NOISE REDUCTION

Noise reduction devices (of which the Dolby system was the first) are generally (but not exclusively) associated with reducing background noise on recorded sound. The system identifies low signal levels and boosts them on recording, leaving the higher levels untouched. The low levels are then attentuated on playback taking the background noise below its original point.

The range of Dolby systems produced over the years is as follows:

Dolby A – designed for use with recording studio 15ips tape machines

Dolby B – either available as individual systems or built in to cassette decks

Dolby Stereo – designed to enhance cinema sound by utilising Dolby A on the encoded print, enhancing frequency response and adding stereo to optional prints

Dolby SR – designed to reduce both noise and distortion on analogue recorders enabling them to compete with digital devices.

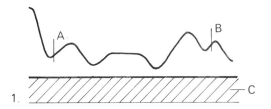

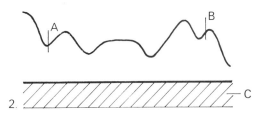

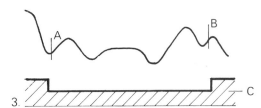

DOLBY 'A' NOISE REDUCTION
In the first drawing the sounds between A and B are close to the background noise level in C. Therefore on recording the A to B sounds are boosted (2) and then attenuated on playback (3) thus reducing the background level.

TIME DELAY SYSTEMS

In a large auditorium, the amplified sound may arrive at the listener before the direct, unamplified sound. It has been found that if the difference in arrival times is greater than 35ms, then the resulting overall sound will be blurred causing a loss to the intelligibility. If the times differ by more than 100ms then there will be a distinct echo. The answer to these problems is to effect an electronic delay to the amplified sound.

The standard text on delay problems was published in 1947 by a Dr Haas; in it he stated that he found that the listener related the direction of the source to that of the sound which arrived first rather than to the sound which was louder. The delay therefore is usually arranged so that the amplified sound arrives after the direct sound, thereby focusing attention on the real source. This is now called the Haas effect and it is the basis for the Deltastereophony system mentioned earlier (although many delay systems do not use Deltastereophony).

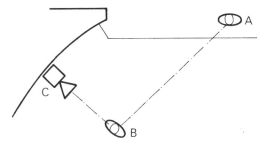

HAAS EFFECT
The sound from the loudspeaker C is delayed so that the live sound from A arrives at B first, the brain then 'moves' the amplified sound to match the direction from which the live sound came.

In a large auditorium it may be necessary to have several sets of time delay loudspeakers because the time difference between different parts of the auditorium might be longer than 35ms. On plan, the calculations are fairly straightforward since the speed of sound in air at a temperature of 14 degrees centigrade is III5' (340m) per second, rising or falling 2ft (0.61m)

Digital delay line.

per second for each degree centigrade. Thus a time of 35ms represents a distance of just under 40′ (12.2m) at this temperature. Hence the differences in the lengths of sound paths from listener to loudspeaker and live source (or other loudspeakers) should be within 40′. Delays can still be useful to enhance the sound where the path differences are below 40′ but delays are essential where the path differences are greater than 40′. The brain's ability to 'move' the sound does not, however, suggest that delay loudspeakers can be positioned anywhere, the same laws apply whether the loudspeaker is delayed or not.

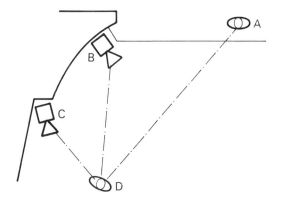

In auditoria with a second pair of speakers beyond the boxes it is necessary to install a second delay line so that the sound CD does not arrive before that of BD. To maintain that directional effect the AD sound should arrive first.

The delay unit is positioned before the amplifier in the chain. Its use involves expense additional to that of the delay unit itself because extra amplifiers and loudspeakers are usually necessary because the use of delay frequently involves extra loudspeaker/amplifier circuits and less 'grouping'. In a correctly tuned delay system the audience should be unaware that amplification is being employed. All delay systems should be capable of being by-passed. The reason for this is that many delay loudspeakers are located in the mid or rear auditorium areas where they might also be useful for sound effects when not being used for vocal work.

ECHO AND REVERBERATION DEVICES – EFFECTS BOXES

A good mixer possesses an auxiliary control on each input channel to route a selected amount of that channel to an external echo unit from where sound is returned to the mix at the group channel. There is a distinction between a reverberation unit and an echo unit. The reverberation unit extends the depth of the last syllable in each word whereas the echo unit causes the whole word to be repeated. Used carefully these devices can add depth to vocal mix especially in a non-reverberent auditorium. The advantage is that the amount of echo is decided by the operator not by the acoustic. In most musical presentations some slight reverberation is desirable, but it should only noticed by its sudden absence if turned off.

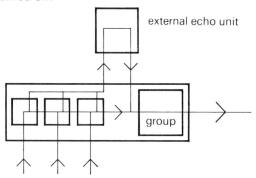

Echo routing from each channel to an external device and then back into the mixer at the group stage.

It is possible to produce some reverberation by feeding the sound into a lively room, i.e. a cloakroom and picking up the resultant direct and reflected sounds by a mic at the other end. In a suitable room this is quite an acceptable effect, but the neighbourhood has to be kept quiet or else embarrassing events (like the sound of a flushing toilet) can be relayed to the audience!

Today many effects, including the distortion favoured by rock musicians, can be produced electronically from devices which can be inserted into the mixer or added elsewhere in the chain. Quite frequently these devices offer a range of facilities including digital delay and most offer memory functions for effects which need to be repeated.

LOUDSPEAKERS

There is perhaps no other area of sound equipment which causes as much controversy as the placing of the loudspeaker. This is because many people are ignorant of the fact that a loudspeaker possesses a specific 'beam'; a known pattern of horizontal and vertical angles of the radiation of the sound. The loudspeaker requires careful positioning and aiming in the same way that a spotlight does. In the next section we shall deal in more detail with positioning loudspeakers but first let us look at the way loudspeakers work; we shall concern ourselves with two main types, the moving coil or direct radiator and the horn or compression driver.

There are two sections which make up the moving coil loudspeaker; the unit which provides the movement itself, often called the cone or driver, and the cabinet or baffle which harnesses and projects the sound. The driver consists of a magnet which is specially shaped to concentrate the field at the suspension point of a coil of wire which is in turn connected to the amplifier. The actual loudspeaker cone is then mounted onto the coil so that it moves backwards and forwards as the magnetic field generated by the sound signal interacts with that of the main magnet.

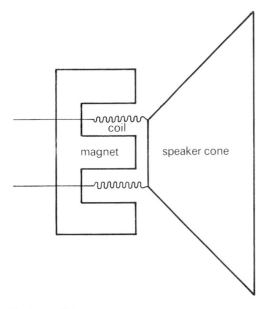

Moving coil loudspeaker.

The performance of a loudspeaker cannot be judged by that of the cone alone since its housing can emphasise or de-emphasise much of the sound. The problem is most apparent at the low frequencies where the long wavelengths can bend round the cone and cancel each other out and as a result the sound is lacking in bass. The cone cannot be mounted on a board (baffle) alone, because the wavelengths of extreme low frequencies are so large, 22′ (6.7m), that they would bend round the ends of the baffle unless it was more than 22′ long! (However an LF unit, in its cabinet, can be built into the structure of the building and can both utilise the vibrations and the planes of the structure to enhance the radiation of the sound, this is known as bass-coupling.)

The cones are enclosed in cabinets which are heavily absorbent inside. A lack of absorption creates too much bass because of the resonance (sympathetic vibrations) of the air inside the cabinet. Most professional units have vented cabinets which are carefully designed so that the sound from the interior emerges in phase with that directly radiated outside and therefore it is reinforced. The design of such enclosures is very much a specialised subject and computers have proved very useful in recent years in calculating how compact an enclosure can be for a given performance.

It may be recalled that low frequencies are omnidirectional and that high frequencies are unidirectional and therefore the 'beam' of the loudspeaker changes with the frequency, the lowest frequencies radiate in all directions; the middle frequencies radiate mostly at the front of the loudspeaker in a 180 degree angle, and the high frequencies radiate at the front of the loudspeaker but progressively less than 180 degrees as the frequency rises. A good manufacturer therefore quotes radiation patterns for specific frequencies so that these beams can be drawn on a theatre plan in order to calculate the best position for the loudspeaker, see for example Table 8 on the following page. The figures should always be quoted with reference to a specific sound pressure level measured in front of the speaker with a stated power input. Generally the beam angle is taken as the boundary at which the sound pressure level falls 6dB from that measured on the axis at 1 metre to the unit, hence the beam angle is also (and more commonly) known as the '6dB down point'.

Table 8

	vertical angle	horizontal angle
1000Hz	180°	113°
2000Hz	128°	130°
4000Hz	86°	112°
8000Hz	70°	116°
16000Hz	50°	102°

frequency response = 50–18000Hz
SPL 1 watt 1 metre pink noise = 101dB

The problem with a single moving coil loud-speaker, a point source, is that the sound is dispersed indiscriminately so that reflections from side walls of the auditorium can reduce intelligibility and also push the system closer to feedback. Point source designs also follow the Inverse Square Law that the sound pressure level falls 6dB everytime the distance is doubled from the source, therefore sound levels set at a rear stalls control desk might be unacceptable nearer the stage nearer to the loudspeaker. An alternative loudspeaker design, the line source column speaker, overcomes these latter two problems to a certain extent and its slim lines often make it easier to conceal.

In the line source column, several cones are mounted vertically and the full power is fed only to the centre cones, less to those above and below the centre, then less again and so on. This produces a very directional beam which makes it ideal for theatre work. The technique is known as power tapering.

Quality line source column showing the HF unit in the centre, note how the moving coil drivers are aimed towards the centre to minimise the vertical dispersion angle.

One problem is that if the high frequencies are produced by all the cones in the column then the resultant beam will be much narrower than those of lower frequencies and therefore some people might not receive the full frequency response. For this reason good columns either feed the high frequencies to the centre cones only – or two columns are constructed side by side within the same cabinet, one for high and one for low.

In another form of tapering the full power is fed to the top cones and then progressively less down the height until the bottom cones receive the least power. This produces less variation in the beam angles with frequency (except for those in the very immediate vicinity).

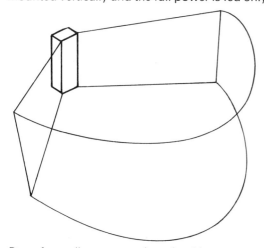

Beam from a line source column is wide horizontally and narrow vertically.

Data for a line source column might look like this:

Table 9

	horizontal angle	vertical angle
1000Hz	115°	30°
2000Hz	90°	60°
4000Hz	110°	70°
8000Hz	118°	70°

frequency response	= 60–16000Hz
SPL 1 watt 1 metre pink noise	= 92dB

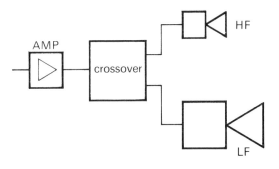

Notice how the beam angle alters with frequency and the 'wedge of cheese' shape is created at the lower frequencies, this can be useful to avoid unwanted reflections.

The vertical line of speakers sets up a different kind of sound wave to that of the point source speaker and the sound pressure level does not fall by 6dB every time the distance is doubled, in fact with a good column there is only a few dB fall off at all. This means that if good columns are used an operator can comfortably set sound levels at the rear of the house in the knowledge that the front rows are not likely to suffer from much higher levels. In fact line source columns are rarely used in theatre work because they lack both sufficient power and a good wide frequency response but the principles of line source design is used especially in large arenas where a column is built of several point-source loudspeakers; these constructions, sometimes 20' high, are known as 'stacks'.

In the moving coil loudspeaker the diameter of the cone relates to the frequencies which it can accurately reproduce and therefore a single cone cannot be expected to authentically produce the whole range of sounds. The solution to this problem is to utilise several cones of differing diameters, each dealing with a different part of the audio band. There would usually be at least two cones; one for the bass (known as the woofer, or more commonly LF driver or bass driver) and one for the treble (known as the tweeter or more commonly HF driver). In these cases a crossover is needed to split the signal so that the LF and HF sounds are routed to their correct loudspeakers.

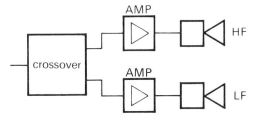

The crossover shown here is after the amplifier in the chain, it is better to place crossovers before the amplifers so that the HF and LF sounds can be cleaner and better balanced.

It is possible to add another loudspeaker with its crossover set for the middle frequencies, this is desirable for systems which deal with a high vocal content since it means that one loudspeaker will handle the main vocal frequencies. If the sound system lacks a middle loudspeaker then the crossover between LF and HF is likely to fall in the vocal range and the sound will not be as smooth.

Generally the diameter of speaker cones will range from I8" to 3" (0.46 to 0.08m) with I2"–6" (0.31 to 0.15m) being the most common. A speaker cone I8" diameter can go down to 15Hz and one 12" can go down to 40Hz. (Extreme low frequency systems can now be produced, these are known as sub-basses.) Alternatively a system for restricted use, say for speech only, could quite acceptably utilise cones 4" (0.10m) diameter which produce frequencies down to 100Hz.

Crossover frequencies between LF and HF are normally at 300–500Hz, and if a mid unit is employed then the LF crossover point might be lower than 300Hz and there would be other crossover points to HF at 1000Hz, 5kHz and 10kHz. Where several LF and HF drivers are mounted within the same cabinet then the crossover could be mounted with them but it is more common for crossovers to be mounted with the amplifiers because the LF and HF loudspeakers are usually in separate cabinets, often not adjacent. Although the mounting of two or three drivers within one cabinet is simpler and could require only one amplifier (if the crossover is built in) it is preferable to place the crossover before the amplifier and feed each driver separately. This is known as bi-amplification and because it permits the LF and HF (and mid where applicable) to be separately balanced the overall sound can be cleaner.

Crossovers can be either set at a fixed frequency (passive) or offer a variety of alternatives (active). An active crossover is particularly beneficial in helping to overcome feedback since it can feed more signal to the directional HF system and away from the omni-directional LF system.

Another function of an active crossover is to protect the HF driver from being overdriven by high sound levels, this is achieved by processor controlling the crossover so that some HF signal is diverted to the LF driver when high levels are detected. High sound levels are common today, especially in rock music which can also generate frequent changes of pure tones. The combination of the two influences can generate fast and excessive movements of the coil so that it burns out or deforms with consequent loss of quality. Despite the protection circuits which some loudspeaker manufacturers offer (the limiting circuits in amplifiers and the processor controlled crossovers) many system designers opt for a horn loudspeaker (sometimes called a compression driver) to produce the high frequencies.

In the horn loudspeaker the coil is attached to a metal diaphragm which excites the air in front of it at a position called the throat. This is in turn connected to the horn itself. The compressed volume of air in the throat reacts quickly and efficiently to the movements of the diaphragm and horn loudspeakers can be up to 50 times more efficient than moving coil designs and their sound pressure level remains relatively constant with distance. However HF horns cannot handle low frequencies because the long wavelengths

involved would require an enormous horn construction, hence HF horns are used in conjunction with crossovers and LF moving coil loudspeakers to produce the complete audio spectrum.

The shape of the horn can be either circular or rectangular. It is the latter which is most suited to theatre working, since this gives the horizontal and vertical beam we require and some rectangular horns also have several 'cells' which improves the dispersion, especially in the middle frequencies. A circular horn gives a conical beam which might have too wide a vertical angle, and this could produce unwanted reflections from the ceiling. Horns can also be provided with a variety of beam shaping devices, vanes, (these are often called lenses) which can limit the upper part of the throw and concentrate more sound down onto the audience. It is because of this precision in the beam that the combination of variable crossovers and HF horn reduces feedback at the lower frequencies. Feedback can occur when the less defined beam of the moving coil loudspeaker directs more sound back to the microphones, hence an adjustment of the crossover routes more signal to the directional horn. Finally some HF horns offer a very uniform beam over all their rated frequencies and do not become progressively narrower as the frequency increases; these units are known as constant directivity horns.

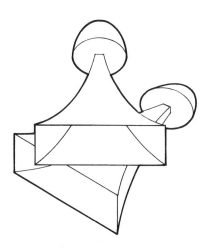

Mounting the horns on top of each other creates a beam similar to that of a line source column, wide horizontally and narrow vertically.

HF and mid range horns showing useful rectangular mouth which creates precise horizontal and vertical beams.

There is another design of loudspeaker which incorporates both the elements we have discussed so far, namely a conventional moving coil bass unit with a horn for the higher freqencies, and all assembled within one cabinet. The advantage of this technique is that the most suitable units for each frequency band are assembled as compactly as possible. Many loudspeakers designed this way are of the best quality available and are used in recording studios to listen to the product when colouration is not permitted, in this case they are known as monitors. Some people use these in theatre work because of their quality, however the HF horn is rarely large enough to offer the kind of precision

A selection of high quality monitors clearly showing the moving coil LF driver and HF horn.

of larger designs and so these monitors behave as point source designs (with the sound level falling off 6dB with every doubling of the distance). This suggests that they are unsuitable for large auditoria. A variation on this theme can be found in some high-quality line-source columns which incorporate a small HF horn in the centre of the moving coil drivers.

The term monitor is also used to denote a loudspeaker which is supplying information to dressing rooms or musicians on stage and not supplying the programme to the audience. In this case the quality of the loudspeaker is not likely to be as high as the studio monitor mentioned above. Generally monitors on stage are used to provide foldback to the artists and in order to minimise their outline and aim the higher frequencies to the artists the loudspeakers are constructed in characteristic wedge shape, typically they are known as 'wedgies' or 'wedge monitors'.

Wedge shaped foldback loudspeakers.

Another recent development is the production of extremely compact loudspeakers specifically designed to handle the vocal frequencies (which we saw earlier can be produced from a 4" diameter cone) and which can be easily hidden in the auditorium, typical uses are for mid-auditorium delay units or front stalls fill from the orchestra rail. Many of these designs are provided with separate bass units which can either be positioned elsewhere (since the low frequencies will find their way anywhere) or on occasions omitted altogether if the main system's bass response is acceptable.

LOUDSPEAKER EFFICIENCY

We have indicated that some speakers are more efficient than others and obviously this is a measure of their ability to provide power and most people are familiar with the measurement in watts (as a product of the voltage and the current flowing). Whilst this indicates how powerful an amplifier needs to be to drive such a loudspeaker, it does not indicate how much power is converted into sound. Measuring loudspeaker performance in watts has been compared to measuring a car's performance by the capacity of the petrol tank rather than by the car's consumption.

A more useful figure for comparing speaker performances is that of the sound pressure level – SPL. This tells us how much sound is produced at a given distance from the unit – for a given input power – and the information is provided in dB in a way that makes it easy to calculate what the SPL would be at say the back of the theatre, since with point source systems doubling the distance decreases the SPL by 6dB each time. The SPL is usually measured fairly near to the speaker, say 3' (1m) and at 1 watt input; these figures should be quoted in relevant data because a SPL reading on its own is meaningless.

Since doubling the wattage produces a 3dB increase in SPL we can therefore work out how many watts need to be supplied in order to produce a certain output from the loudspeaker.

For example if a loudspeaker produced 90dB at 4' from 1 watt then the following would apply:

from 1	watt input we get a SPL of 90dB at 4'
2	93
4	96
8	99
16	102
32	105
64	108

If we now apply the 6dB/distance rule we can therefore work out what the SPL would be at the back of the auditorium, say 64' away from the loudspeaker, thus:

108dB is provided at	4' (with 64 watt input)
102	8'
96	16'
90	32'
84	64'

84dB is acceptable perhaps for speech reinforcement (especially taking into account the contribution from other loudspeakers and the environment) but it would not be acceptable for higher levels of amplification such as those associated with musicals and rock. In fact suppose that our target SPL at 64' was 100dB then we would have to supply considerably more wattage to produce that level from this loudspeaker:

from 64	watts input we get a SPL of 84dB at 64'
128	87
256	90
512	93
1024	96
2048	99

A more efficient loudspeaker than the one above would save considerable power (and money!). So firstly let us calculate what SPL we need at 4' in order to produce 100dB at 64':

at 64' the desired SPL is 100dB	
32'	106
16'	112
8'	118
4'	124

Using a more efficient loudspeaker we can now calculate how much power could be needed to produce 124dB at 4'. Our more efficient loudspeaker produces 112dB at 4' from 1 watt, therefore:

from 1	watt input we get a SPL of 112dB at 4'
2	115
4	118
8	121
16	124

Clearly the second loudspeaker is the more desirable. The above calculations do not take into account any available headroom. Suppose that it was thought that 12dB of headroom was needed then we can continue the second loudspeaker calculations to find out how much power would be needed to reach the headroom SPL of 136dB (124+12).

from 16	watts input we get a SPL of 124dB at 4'
32	127
64	130
128	133
256	136

So assuming that the loudspeaker could accept 256 watts we would need an amplifier producing say 300 watts to achieve the desired programme level of 100dB with the designed headroom of 12dB. Rock musicians frequently work with a headroom of 30dB which would require 1000 watts extra power; since amplifiers produce more power at lower impedances many rock system designers prefer to work at 4 ohm rather than 8 ohm (and at the time of writing there is evidence of a move to 2 ohm systems). It is useful for a moment to consider the voltages and currents employed here. If we recall our earlier equation:

$$volts^2 = watts \times ohms$$

then   1000 watts $\times$ 8 ohms $= 89.44$ volts
(11.18 amps)

but at 4 ohms...

1000 watts $\times$ 4 ohms $= 63.24$ volts
(15.81 amps)

Hence lowering the impedance increases the current and connectors and cable have to take that into account.

Some loudspeakers are designed to work with their own equalisers which do even out the peaks and troughs in the unit's performance. Since this technique can produce a flatter frequency response than would otherwise be expected from a given diameter and selection of cones, loudspeakers which utilise this approach can be surprisingly compact in relationship to their output. However the extra boost at the

Very popular loudspeaker which uses its own equaliser to enhance the response, its output is considerable in relationship to its size and its rugged construction is useful when touring.

upper and lower frequencies is achieved through drawing extra power from the amplifier and this must be taken into account in the overall system design. The equaliser used is also not adjustable and is not an alternative for a graphic, although if a loudspeaker produces a flatter response then there is less need for a graphic to be employed unless the auditorium introduces some particular emphasis which needs reducing.

So the above formula can only be a guide because of a number of factors which must be taken into account:

a) line source designs do not follow the 6dB (Inverse Square Law) rule

b) point source designs should be mounted at equal distances from all seats so that the fall off is the same for all

c) the auditorium's natural reverberation also adds to the final sound pressure level

d) each time the number of loudspeakers delivering the same programme is doubled then the overall sound pressure level increases by 3dB

Here are some typical SPL figures for various loudspeaker types:

Table 10

	1 watt at 10'	full power at 4'
HF horn	105dB	133dB
line source column	88dB	115dB
studio monitor	97dB	125dB

The efficiency of the HF horn is clear from these figures, but it is also clear that all would be suited to the application described above although the HF horn could not be used alone, requiring a bass unit to complete the system. In the past it was rare for English speaker manufacturers to quote such data but now they follow earlier guidelines laid down by those in the United States.

Table 11
Sound pressure level of typical horn loudspeakers with 1 watt at 1 metre

unit 1 ——	3500Hz–15kHz plus/minus 4dB ——————	101dB
unit 2 ——	3500Hz–15kHz plus/minus 3dB ——————	104dB
unit 3 ——	3500Hz–15kHz plus/minus 2dB ——————	107dB
unit 4 ——	1000Hz–3500Hz plus/minus 3dB ——————	103dB
unit 5 ——	800Hz–3500Hz plus/minus 3dB ——————	105dB

As above the SPL should relate to a specific frequency band for more valuable comparisons.

It can be seen from this comparison that unit 3 has the flattest response and the highest output but choice also rests on the beam angle. For comparison a moving coil loudspeaker might have a response 40Hz – 16kHz plus/minus 4dB with SPL 89dB 1 watt 1 metre.

SUMMARY

A single speaker cone is incapable of producing all the desired audio band accurately and therefore there are different sizes of cones for bass, mid and treble frequencies each of which is routed via a crossover. These devices may be set at specific frequency points or they may be variable which assists in reducing feedback and protects the HF coil.

Speaker cones can be mounted in line vertically, this design produces little fall-off of sound pressure level with distance and in this format they also produce distinctly shaped beams which are useful in theatre work.

Moving coil loudspeakers are not efficient and are prone to damage if asked to handle high sound levels at high frequencies. A horn speaker can handle these levels and it is also efficient and very directional. A good wide range system might have several bass 'bins' with mid and high-frequency horns. Column speakers have been improved recently but would be unable to offer as wide a frequency range as the bass bin/HF horn system.

The performance of loudspeakers should be measured in dB as an indication of the sound pressure level produced at a given distance for a given input and ideally this should be expressed for different frequencies. The beam of the speaker should also be quoted relevant to a specific SPL and frequency. This information is vital in designing a sound system in order to accurately predict how loud the system will be and what is the best position for the loudspeaker.

CONNECTIONS AND CABLING

The reader will by now be familiar with the concept of the sound chain and will be conscious that any piece of equipment which is incompatible with the rest becomes the weak link. The cabling and connections of the sound system are also links in the chain but the installation is not glamorous; unlike impressive mixers and control rooms it cannot be shown off – indeed it frequently causes the decor to be repainted and it is often untidy. Since out-of-sight means out-of-mind, the installation is often omitted from the budget, causing its later inclusion to be carried out at cut-price. This is false economy because sound systems rely on small connections and since sound signals are weak by comparison with the strengths of other electrical currents in theatres they are prone to interference. The installation must therefore be taken seriously.

BALANCED AND UNBALANCED LINES

An unbalanced line is that most commonly (but not exclusively) associated with domestic equipment and it consists of a single wire plus a shield which is earthed, the voltage between the two is the signal. This system is prone to interference and is rarely employed in professional equipment in preference to balanced lines. In this system there are two signal carrying conductors plus a shield. One conductor is positive, the other negative and so any interference effects both parts of the signal and is cancelled out.

INSTALLATION

Mic and the line level cables should have twin conductors and they should be enclosed in a braided screen and then in metal conduit or trunking. On no account should mic or line level wiring be taken nearer than 200mm (say 8") to mains cabling. Long parallel runs of mics and mains (or speakers) are not desirable and they should cross each other only where necessary, and then only at 90 degrees. On no account should mic or line level cabling (or sound equipment in general) be positioned near to main switchgear or other electrical equipment with a potentially strong 'field', or near to thyristor dimming equipment.

Today there are many excellent manufacturers offering multicore mic cable (where several mic circuits are encased within one overall protective sheath) and it is usual to design the installation around the cable choice; multicore is easier to install than a lot of individual lines and often can be better protected. This technique has meant that mic outlets are collected into boxes in key locations rather than spread out individually all over the performing area. The number of ways in each box ('stage left box', 'orchestra box' for example) being linked to the appropriate choice of multicore, thus one talks of 'twelve way boxes' being served by a twelve way (12 circuit) multicore. It is wise to add other lines designated 'tie lines' between the stage and control positions, these allow flexibility when visiting companies bring their own equipment or when tape decks and mixers need to be repositioned, perhaps on stage, and line level signals need to be sent to different parts of the building.

Loudspeaker signals are stronger than mic or line levels and therefore less susceptible to interference. Nevertheless they must be treated with respect. Speaker cables have two conductors only, which must be colour coded (and ideally twisted to cancel any interference). The diameter of the conductor depends upon the load and on the cable length, too small a cable and there will be too great a loss of signal, this is inevitable to some extent and is called the 'damping factor'; it can be calculated so that the loss of amplifier power is not significant.

The Association of British Theatre Technicians publishes this guide:

Table 12

8 ohm, 50m up to 100w	0.75 mm²
8 ohm, 50m, 100w to 400w	2.50 mm²
8 ohm, 50m, 400w to 1000w	4.00 mm²
100v line, up to 100w	0.50 mm² (paging only)
100v line, 100w to 1000w	1.00 mm² (paging only)

Speaker cable does not need to be run in conduit or trunking but it is a good idea to do so. Some local authorities require that 100v line cable is run in metal conduit. Loudspeaker runs should be clear of mains and mic level cables and all sound cables should take a different route than mains and thyristor lighting cabling from stage to the control position.

CONNECTORS

There is still some controversy on this matter and therefore conflicting standards can be found. Generally, the profession is agreed on mic connectors but not on speaker connectors.

Firstly only a metal covered connector will withstand the battering that theatres can offer.

The standard XLR connectors for microphones.

All mic connections are of the 3-pin variety (typically Cannon and there are several equivalent makes now available). In the past jacks were unpopular because they could not withstand the punishment of the Cannon and frequently came unplugged with prolonged use, they were therefore restricted to the patch panel. However more recent designs are not only more durable but are also fitted with latching devices like the Cannon connectors so that they do not come unplugged,

Rear view of a mixer showing female connectors for mic inputs and male connectors for outputs.

despite this it would be sensible to retrict jacks to the control area and remain with Cannons for the stage area.

Mic level signal carriers are male, which carry even numbers on the Cannon XLR scale. They have a 3 pins for the shield and two conductors, thus a plug on a cable would be XLR – 3 – 12c whereas a panel mounted plug would be XLR – 3 – 32. The earth is connected to pin 1, positive conductor to pin 2, and negative conductor to pin 3. If any microphone does not work well it is worth checking the polarity because, faulty wired apart, some imported designs can be wired in a different way.

Speaker connectors can be jacks but Cannons are more popular, they are tougher and can carry the high current associated with big loudspeaker systems. Some time ago 4-pin Cannons were recommended since this accommodated both 100v line and low impedance systems on one connector – both requiring two pins each. However as sound levels grew, so did the current and many people linked pins together, confusion reigned and this practice is now rare. There is still no standard and both 3-pin Cannon and EP

connectors are popular but there is now a specially designed loudspeaker connector (the Neutric) which provides 4 contacts for bi-amplification and which can be rated up to 30amp RMS for powering large systems.

EDAC multiway connectors typically used for mixer inputs and outputs.

Mixer inputs and outputs, and other items of equipment where there is a large quantity of connections to make, are best terminated in multicore plugs and sockets. Not only do these take up far less room than the Cannons (and the multicore will be smaller than individual lines) but they are easier to handle and less prone to mistaken cross plugging.

If finance permits it is sensible to terminate all lines and equipment in a jackfield in the control area, thus different configurations can be 'patched'. It is true that most equipment is provided with plugs and sockets on the rear so some alteration in format is always possible but it is not wise to move equipment or cabling constantly. Jacks can suffer from poor connections after prolonged use and so only the very best quality

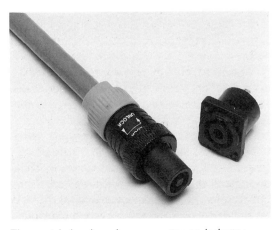

The neutric loudspeaker connector; an industry standard at last?

designs should be considered. Most professional jackfields are 'normalled'; this means that the signal involved follows a 'normal' route unless it is interrupted by the insertion of the jackplug. In this way the jackfield can offer considerable flexibility.

Mixer showing in-built jackfield under the desk.

MAINS SUPPLIES

The most important requirement for mains supplies for sound equipment is that they should separate from all others in the building. This means being separate in such a way that disturbances in other supplies caused by contactors on heating and ventilation systems cannot effect the sound systems. Mains supplies free of such disturbances are known as 'dedicated', it is especially important that the earth is clean, and an alternative title is 'clean feed' or 'dedicated earth'. Since computers (used in the box office or accounting) also need dedicated earths it is important to stress than the sound system must have its own. It is possible to insert a mains filter into the system which not only suppresses mains noise but also filters out lighting and control

interference, however since the devices are usually rated for fairly small currents, 6 amps is commonly maximum, several might be required in the system.

The whole house sound system should be fed from a single phase isolator and all plugs and sockets for the equipment should be correctly fused to their load. A liberal number of outlets is desirable, each should have a neon indicator and be engraved 'sound mains only' or otherwise similarly identified and it should not be forgotten that equipment is occasionally positioned in unusual locations and so sockets should be available around the stage, orchestra pit, apron and slips. Additional outlets should be available near equipment racks where test equipment such as oscilloscopes may be used.

A mains distribution panel typically found in equipment racks, the fuse illuminates when it blows.

It is especially important to ensure maximum protection for musicians using electrical instruments; accidents with electric guitars are frequently fatal.

An old method of protection was the provision of an isolating transformer, but this is not effective if several instruments are fed from the same transformer.

Current practice is to provide residual circuit breakers for each instrument (and it is sensible to spread the sockets out for orchestra pit, auditorium and stage). These devices switch off the power when a fault is detected; often the fault is such that the fuse will not blow and earthing is faulty, a potentially lethal situation. The ABTT publishes an excellent leaflet on this subject and advises that each breaker shoud operate at no more than 30 milliamp and not more than 30 milliseconds.

A common problem is the matching of mains connectors on visitors' equipment and the ABTT also advises the provision of outlet boxes, containing the available connectors, 5A, 13A and 15A, and fed through the circuit breakers. This obviates changing plugs which is time consuming and occasionally dangerous where pressure of work can cause carelessness.

It is particularly important to check fuses and connections of all incoming equipment. Touring groups are notoriously lax about safety, and fame is no guarantee of good maintenance. Under the terms of the Health and Safety Act, there are no exclusion causes for theatre managers and their staff.

Many visiting groups require a separate power supply on stage for their own sound system, 100 amp single phase is typical, and a good theatre design will include trunking or traps to permit the control and loudspeaker cabling to reach the front-of-house mixing position tidily.

EARTH LOOPS

In unbalanced lines it is feasible for the shield on one piece of equipment to be earthed in a different way to that on another piece of equipment. The earth loop thus created can pick up interference from mains and from radio transmission of minicabs, police etc. It is a mistake however to assume that a balanced line system could not

suffer from an earth loop so the connection of the shield is still very important. Indeed all mic and line level cables possess earth or shield conductors and all mains cables from equipment does so. It is possible therefore that any cable might be inadvertently connected in such a way that an 'earth loop' is created. Therefore the earth circuit of low level signal items should be arranged so that it is connected to ground only at one point, generally the mixer, with the signal lead carrying the continuity. However it is wise to provide separate grounds for musicians' power supplies and to those for the large loads of the amplifiers. The ground should ideally not be that shared with the lighting system.

This grounding principle applies to any equipment added to a system for however temporary a period because temporary wiring of extra mixers or amplifiers could cause problems with earth loops, as could the connection of some test equipment.

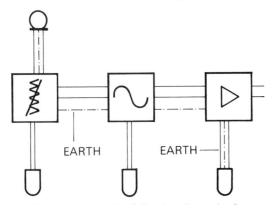

Avoiding earth loops by following the path of shielding to one unit and then from that along to the earth on the mains plug.

SECTION FOUR – SYSTEM DESIGN

Vocals

A cardioid hand mic for vocals needs to be pointed towards the source of the sound. Even experienced performers can lack good microphone technique and since aiming the mic directly towards the mouth is tiring the mic can spend most of its time 'seeing' the mouth at an angle, off axis between the 45 degree through 0 to the 316 degree points on the polar diagrams and the response of the microphone in this position should be carefully checked for colouration.

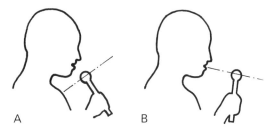

A   B

The performer in B is holding the mic off-axis shown by the dotted line, unless the mics response at 90° and 180° is good the overall sound will be thin and weak; the performer in A is holding the mic closer to its axis point which is far better however it can be tiring to do this for long periods and a good off axis response is therefore important.

If a performer is especially 'lazy' in pointing the mic at his mouth then sometimes an omnidirectinal mic can be substituted for a cardioid. Omnidirectional mics can be of exceptional quality and obliviate many breathing and vocal blasting noises and many designers favour them. (Condenser omnis also have excellent low frequency response which is useful in recording and on miking musical instruments.)

However whilst omnis will improve pickup of a 'lazy' user they will also hear more of the surrounding sounds and it will be harder for the operator to achieve a good vocal separation (omnis could also push the system closer to feedback). All hand mics should be held about 6–8" away from the mouth, performers and operators need to remember that a mic moved from 8" to 4" produces an extra 6dB in level even though the performer has not produced extra level. A related problem is that some performers use so much voice that distortion results at high sound levels (some singers produce 120dB or more at these times) and once present distortion is almost impossible to eradicate and so the singer blames the system or its operator.

Some performers will move the mic away when about to produce a high level, it is often easier for them to effect corrections of this nature than a new sound operator (though he needs to know the work equally well) however dramatic fluctuations are disturbing and it is wiser to ensure that there is sufficient headroom for occasional peaks without the operator (or the performer) having to make constant adjustments.

Some singers use the mic close enough to cause 'blasting' on the plosive consonants – 'p', 'b', 't', 's' and most mics will take an additional component – a breath filter or 'pop gag' to cut out these blasting sounds. These filtering devices may be either metal or foam and their selection and use should be considered carefully, since some filters can reduce the sensitivity of the mic's pickup to high freqencies when used on musical instruments. This may not be critical if the loudspeaker system is incapable of reproducing those frequencies anyway but ideally the filter should be removable.

Performers are sensitive about types of mics, and it is often a good idea to try out a selection (most mics can be hired by the day) to find out which produces the best sound and which feels right in the performer's hand. Different acoustics might also require different mics – a fact to remember when on tour although the chances of a performer making such changes are unlikely. Mics should be tested by speaking or singing and not by counting.

General Pickup and Amateur Shows

In most reinforcement applications the requirement is to pick up voices all over the stage. This is sadly becoming more frequent in drama as actors become more accustomed to working in television and less trained to project their voices, but the major professional usage for amplification would be on productions where music is employed for example, musicals, pantomimes and light entertainment.

With untrained voices reinforcement will probably be unavoidable. However in such cases there is often a greater range of vocal projection between the performers than is the case (in theory at least!) in professional productions, and in amateur shows the experienced regular will be side by side with the enthusiastic newcomer. Therefore general reinforcement simply makes that range more noticeable to the audience. Usually amateur shows not only need to be provided with general pickup for chorus etc, but also to be provided with selective pickup for the principals (on which they are more likely to rely) by means of radio and rifle mics. This way the range of voices can be better balanced at the mixer. This kind of system is coming closer to that of the professional shows perhaps because the range of voices is coming closer too. Even in opera today there is reinforcement by concealed mics (they are also used for offstage chorus and instruments).

One technique often used in general pickup is the suspension of mics over the stage but since much of the voice's clarity is high frequency, and therefore directional, much of the clarity will be lost if the mic points straight down. However a rifle mic can be aimed at an angle, say from the number one spotbar area to mid or upstage. In this format it will 'see' the mouth at an angle and obtain a better pickup than an ordinary cardioid pointing straight down. It is worth noting that rifles used in this way might still need some extra equalisation at the mixer to restore the useful middle frequencies which the rifle mic has not picked up too successfully.

An omnidirectional mic hanging straight down is useful where information and not quality is important, as in the case of show relay to dressing rooms although many show relay mics are also used to feed the hard-of-hearing loop where quality is important and in which case they are more likely to be cardioids mounted to face the stage from boxes and lighting bridges.

The usual position for general pickup mics is in

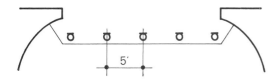

Microphone spacing across the footlights, the mics in the corners could be omitted if there is no action in that part of the stage.

the footlights' trough along the edge of the stage. An odd number is helpful since this means there will be one centre stage – an important acting area. Ideally the mics should be no more than 5' (1.52m) apart otherwise a 'hole' might appear in the response as a performer walks across; measure the proscenium and divide by 5', the nearest odd number will be the number of mics needed although usually the corner areas are not important and these can be omitted, hence a 36' (11m) proscenium would have five mics. On small stages where performers are obliged to work very close to the front edge it is wise to mount the float mics off the vertical edge and out of the dancers' way! Condenser mics are more popular in the footlights because they are more sensitive. All float mics should be cardioid and some people prefer to use a small gun having a hypercardioid response; more gain before feedback being the aim. Another advantage of this format is the rejection of sound from the orchestra pit, especially useful if the pit contains a high percentage of electronic instruments. This method also probably has the edge over mounting the cardioid pickup capsule on short extention tubes (to get closer to the actors) which is unsightly. Other designers use ordinary cardioids and point them at the stage floor where the direct and reflected sounds will not arrive at different times and cancel each other out (as they could if the mic was pointed higher at the artist) but will arrive together and reinforce each other. To achieve this condenser float mics are often provided with grey foam rubber mounts, in this format they are known as 'mice'.

Pointing ordinary cardioids at the floor does not work if carpets are used since there is no reflecting surface, under these circumstances the short gun mic would probably be the more useful. However a relatively new microphone design, the pressure zone mic, or boundary mic, could be an alternative since it carries with it a small section of reflective surface. The PZM consists of a condenser mic mounted on a small plate which collects the reflections. The basic mic has a hemispherical pickup pattern and hence this would generally exclude its use from the floats where the pickup would also include orchestra and audience. (There may also be other locations where this pickup is too general.)

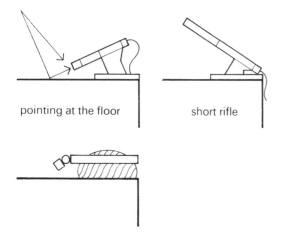

pointing at the floor

short rifle

A boundary or pressure zone mic with omni-directional pickup area.

FLOATMICS
A mic pointed at the floor often produces more level than one directed at the actors. A condenser mic can be fitted with a small swivel tube to enable the pickup capsule to be directed at the floor.

However it is possible to attach a transparent shield which will limit the pick up area and new designs are also being produced with cardioid pickups, known as phase coherent cardioids. For other uses the PZM mic need not be fixed to a surface since it carries its own surface with it, thus it could be mounted on a stand, suspended in the air or concealed in the set (useful in opera and situations where a little amount of reinforcement is needed). The pickup response of a pzm is increased 6dB with every additional plane, hence mounted against one surface the response goes up 6dB (by comparison with the response in free air), in the corner between two surfaces the response goes up by 12dB and in the apex of three surfaces the response goes up by 18dB.

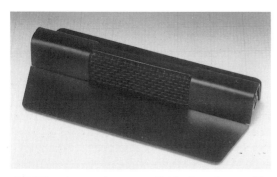

A PCC – *phase coherent cardioid microphone with a supercardioid response, a discrete unit with high output.*

Some sound operators feel that general pickup mics should always be used en masse, so that blanket coverage is maintained. This is clearly nonsense if it is necessary to pick up only one part of the stage. Only the mic serving that part should be used and cross faded to another mic as the performer moves, indeed it is important to understand that every time the number of mics in use is doubled, the effective gain of the system has to be reduced by 3dB or else feedback will result.

MUSICAL INSTRUMENT PICKUP

Outside the recording studio where mics are obviously essential it may be considered that musical instruments produce enough sound level on their own and do not require further amplification. There is some justification for this theory but the miking up of orchestras is often carried out for control of the mix rather than for volume (an amplified violin will not sound like two violins! Special signal processing can achieve this but it lies outside the scope of most systems).

In light entertainment, part of the programme will probably have been popularised by recordings or television, where sophisticated techniques – often with multitrack tape and several 'takes' cut and mixed together – produce the desired sound. To reproduce this in the theatre is difficult but necessary if the stage is the performer's market place for his product and undoubtedly as CD systems become more popular at home so the theatre and club sound systems will have to improve to match the quality.

Stage musicians rarely have the control of their

recording studio counterparts – indeed they are not paid to have – and frequently they change jobs within the life of a production, so some outside cohesive control of the sound is desirable. With each instrument, or section of the orchestra miked up, the sound operator can blend, correct and shape the sound closer to that which the audience are accustomed to hearing at home. Indeed some performers insist on the theatre sound operator and recording studio engineer being the same person. This overcomes the problem of poorly paid operation, and it provides control by a person who knows the most about a performer's work. However such an engineer also needs to know about theatre acoustics and equipment. Fortunately mixing desks in theatre are based on those which originated in studios where the larger budgets and greater technical competition provided growth.

Stage musicians do not always appreciate being controlled from elsewhere and feel that a mic in front of them means that they are not playing loud enough, so they blow harder. It is vital that the whole concept, and the details of miking are discussed with the musicians. They will have their own ideas of the best positions and will often move the mic after the sound engineer has gone. Some musicians express jealousy if they are not miked whilst their neighbours are; the answer is sometimes to provide them with one but not use it! Where musicians are miked up, cardioid microphones should be used because in the close proximity of the orchestra pit the effect would be destroyed if mics picked up generally instead of specifically. Screens are also desirable to prevent some instruments from 'spreading' (notably brass and drums) and occasionally hypercardioid mics have to be selected. It is usually desirable to provide one mic to each instrument. This means that drums are treated as separate items: bass, side, cymbals etc., and not provided with one mic as 'drums'. The position of the mic and its stand should not impede the musician's movements.

The precise choice of mic should take into account the way in which each instrument produces sound since it will need to 'see' the point from which the higher frequencies emerge. The mic will also need to be tailored to the frequency response of the instrument, the bass drum for example produces lower freqencies than most ordinary mics and is best served by a mic which enjoys specially extended low frequency response for this purpose. In fact since most musical instruments generate harmonics going into several thousand hertz, and can have very low fundamentals, mics with a wide range of frequency response are desirable. The response should also be flat as any peaks or troughs desired are brought into effect by the operator, not the system. For these reasons cardioid condensors are desirable but expensive if there are many musicians. A good quality dynamic would be acceptable for most applications – some being produced especially for musical instrument pickup. Manfacturers' literature is usually very helpful on these points.

Amplified instruments such as electric guitars and keyboards can create many balance problems essentially because they are capable of achieving much greater levels than any unamplified instrument. It has been suggested that the sound levels from electronic instruments increase as the run of a production extends, upsetting the balance and other musicians. One problem of much rock music is that part of the sound is created by deliberately driving the system hard in order to produce distortion and overload and this is often achieved alongside high sound levels. In these circumstances the overall quality of the mix can become secondary to the priority given to helping the non-electronic instruments to compete.

One answer is to provide a smaller loudspeaker for the guitar or keyboard (still driven to overload but now without the power), the rest of the amplification being provided by the main system. However this depends upon the musician not selfishly turning up his system during the performance and spoiling the overall mix worked out at rehearsal. It is worth noting that the effects of feedback and distortion desired by many musicians can now be produced electronically from 'trick boxes' via signal processing and need not be created by abusing the sound system at all.

Speech:
C 414, C 535,
* C562 BL, * C567, D 222

Vocal Soloist:
C 414, C 535, C 460 B-ULS,
D 300 Series

Chorus:
C 422, C 34, C 535,
D 300 Series

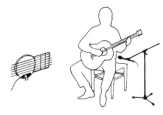

Acoustic Guitar:
C 414, C 460 B-ULS,
* C 567, D 224

E-Guitar:
D 224, D 125

E-Bass:
D 12, D 202 E1,
D222, D 112

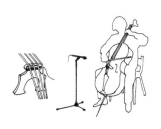

Double Bass:
C 414, C 460 B-ULS,
D 224, *C 567

Cello:
C 414, C 460 B-ULS,
*C 567, D 222

Violin:
C 414, C 460 B-ULS,
*C 567, D 222

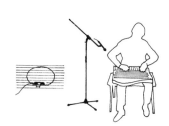

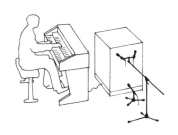

Zither:
C 460 B-ULS,
D 224, *C 567

Leslie Speaker:
Top: 2 × D 224, 2 × D 125
Bottom: D 12, D 112, D 125

Upright Piano:
High's: C 460 B-ULS, D 224
Low's: C 414, D 202 El, *2 × C567

Grand Piano:
High's: C 460 B-ULS, D 224
Low's: C 414, D 202 E1, *2 × C 567

Tuba:
C 414, C 535, *C 567

Horn:
C 414, C 535

Trombone:
C 414, C 535, D 330, D 321

Saxophone:
C 414, C 451 + CK5, C 535,
*C 567, D 300 Series

Trumpet:
C 414,
C 451 + CK5, D 321

Clarinet:
C 414, C 451 + CK5

German Flute:
C 414, C 460, B-ULS,
C 535, *C 567

Mouth Organ:
C 414, C 535, D 300 Series

Snare:
C 460 B-ULS, D 224, D 125

Hi-Hat:
C 460 B-ULS, C 535, D 224

Overhead (Cymbals):
C 414, C 460 B-ULS, C 535
C 568

Bongos:
C 460
B-ULS,
D 224,
D 125

Toms recorded from top:
D 202 E1, D 320, D 321

Congas:
C 460 B-ULS, D 202 E1, D 125

Bass Drum:
D 12, D 202 E1, D 112

Toms recorded from bottom:
D 321, D 320, D 125

MUSICAL INSTRUMENT PICKUP
*Suggestions from AKG as to suitable locations for placing their studio range of microphones for recording musical instruments; the positions are quite acceptable for reinforcement although such high quality mics would not be necessary, others in the AKG range would be acceptable. *For special applications.*

DIRECT INJECTION BOXES *(range of options offered by EMO)*

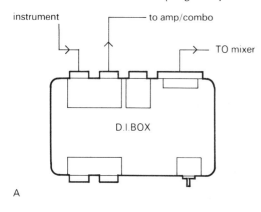

A

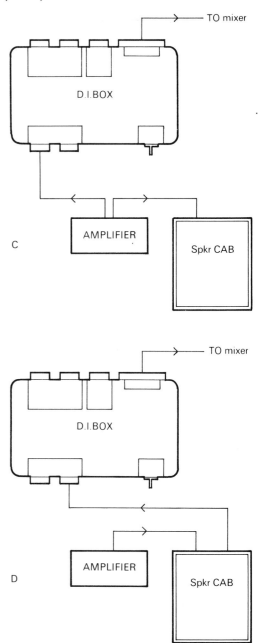

C

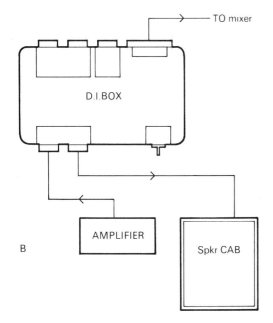

B

D

INSTRUMENT LINE IN

This is a low level signal input (max 1V) having an input impedance of approx. 100K ohms and is suitable for most instrument pick-ups, pianos, etc. The most common connection is shown in A.

L/S LINE IN

This is a high level input (max 100V) suitable for use from loudspeaker lines. Normal connection is as in B, however the unit may be driven from a parallel speaker output from an amplifier C, or from a parallel speaker socket on a loudspeaker cabinet D.

A further method of connecting to this input is as in E.

AMP/SLAVE LINE IN

This is a medium level input (max 30V) for use with slave output sockets on amplifiers and combination amplifiers. This is shown in F. This input will also work from inputs such as mixer outputs (when output isolation is necessary), synthesiser line outputs, etc.

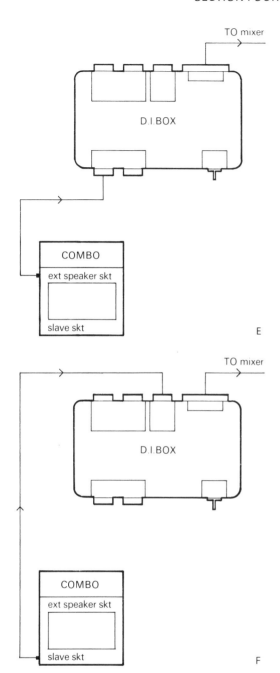

The substitution of direct-injection boxes (commonly known as DI boxes) for instrument microphones also reduces the system's liability to feedback since everytime the number of open microphones is halved then the effective gain of the system can be increased by 3dB. Consider the following band set-up which the author inherited and mixed for a popular group:

mic 1 lead vocal
mic 2 snare
mic 3 bass drum
mic 4 lead guitar
mic 5 bass guitar
mic 6 keyboard 1

The group initially toured with a small six-way mixer and found that in many situations they could not hear the lead vocal over the group and were prevented from achieving a higher level through feedback. By substituting DI boxes for mics 4, 5 and 6 the level of the feedback was reduced, the group's level more controlled and the overall system level increased by exactly 6dB.

In all situations of this nature it is important that all those involved appreciate the balance between the amount of control the musicians themselves want and the maximum gain that the system is capable of offering to the most important mic, generally that for the main vocal. Once maximum gain is reached on the main vocal mic everything else must be pulled down to retain some clarity and separation.

SUMMARY

The brief given to prospective suppliers should indicate the relationship between vocal and instrumental use and so the general direction of microphone choice should be clear. Unless the budget is tight, when a multi-purpose mic would be the most economic, main pickup and vocal mics should be condensers; it will be recalled that these are especially sensitive and produce a good flat response. There is another major advantage in their selection in that many condenser systems are modular, and so a small selection of parts can serve many functions. We have stated that general pickup is achieved by float mics but if the stage is large and action takes

It is wiser that instead of the guitar or keyboard speaker using a mic, a feed is taken from the guitar amp or keyboard straight to the mixer, via a connector box, a process known as direct injection. This can provide more control and a cleaner sound; contact mics using piezo-electric polymers can also be used on musical instruments reducing pickup from other instruments.

place upstage then several rifle mics would be an advantage – for most stages three would be the minimum.

In this case condenser mics are better then dynamics which are far less sensitive (they are also expensive so that hiring might be cheaper). Some PZM or PCM units (perhaps also hired) might be helpful upstage concealed in the set. In addition most stages need at least two hand-mics on long wander leads and these should be purchased even if radio-mics are in use since there will be times when they are needed as standbys.

Orchestral work is also likely on most stages and at least six mics should be provided. Here the choice could easily revert to dynamics, if the budget is tight, since there are many excellent dynamic mics produced specifically for use with musical instruments in order to capture the wide frequency response. Finally in this section there may be some direct injection from keyboards. Based on the above comments the microphone requirement for a small musical might be as the diagram below indicates.

Based on this example the mixer would require at least 24 input channels. This could be reduced with re-patching if some mics were not used all the time, perhaps the PCCs are used only in one set when the handmics are not needed, however re-patching during a show is unwise as it can lead to errors. If the production was not a musical but a straight play requiring general pickup then the vocal and orchestra mics could be omitted and thus the mixer would only require 10 chan-nels. However there are now several instances where straight actors are using concealed radio mics so this must be taken into account as an option.

LOUDSPEAKER POSITIONING

It may be recalled that the high frequencies, which contain the clarity in speech and in music, are very directional and therefore loudspeakers need to be specifically aimed if the clarity is to reach the audience. Because most loudspeakers are rectangular they are easier to fix squarely to a wall rather than to direct at an angle but the temptation to do so must be avoided if this means that the main beam will pass over the audience's heads.

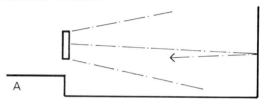

It is tempting to fasten loudspeakers directly to the wall as in A, especially if they are rectangular, however, the main beam passes over the heads of the audience and is reflected from the back wall. The speaker must be aimed to the audience as in B to improve the HF coverage and avoid reflections.

As we saw earlier a good loudspeaker manu-facturer will provide data for the horizontal and vertical beam angles at the 6dB down point and so these beam angles can be drawn on plans and sections in order to select the most suitable loca-

FLOATS......... general pickup 36' pros ...... 5 condenser short rifles

UPSTAGE....... general pickup from no 1 bar. 3 condenser rifles

ONSTAGE ...... concealed in set.............. 2 PCC

VOCALS .... hand held from wings........ 2 dynamic cardioids

PRINCIPALS.... concealed in costume........ 4 radios

ORCHESTRA ... tymps and strings .... 6 dynamic cardioids
keyboards .... 2 direct injection

tion for the loudspeaker and determine the resulting coverage. Some manufacturers offer computer graphics packages which can provide considerable data about a given loudspeaker's performance. The prospective venue is measured and then drawn onto the screen and the computer's mouse then moves the loudspeaker about the room whilst the program provides a read out of the variations of sound pressure levels around the space.

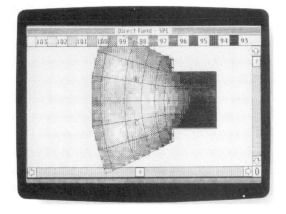

A page from the Bose acoustic modelling program showing SPL's drawn on a sample auditorium plan.

Basic positioning depends on the work which the system has to do and there are two fundamental system types for theatre work. If the sound system is required primarily to amplify or reinforce voices then in most theatres a single loudspeaker system hung centrally over the proscenium arch or acting area is the best choice. In this type of system design the loudspeaker format is known as a centre cluster and the main reason for it being increasingly popular is that a single source will produce fewer reflections from side walls or roof and the resulting sound will be clearer.

Another reason why this system is excellent is that the lengths of the sound paths from the cluster to each audience member will be more uniform than would be the case if the loudspeakers were positioned lower (say at either side of the proscenium) and therefore with centre cluster systems the overall sound pressure level can be more even and there should also be more gain before feedback than with multiple loudspeaker systems. (It has been suggested

that the maximum 'throw' for a cluster should be no more than three times its height above the audience.)

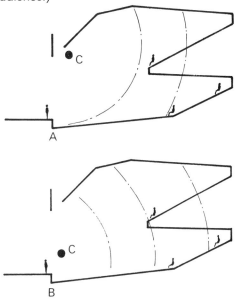

CENTRE CLUSTERS
In A more of the audience is within easy reach of cluster C than is the audience in B within easy reach of speaker C. In B the rear rows would be the more likely to need a delay system to balance out the levels, thus adding to the cost of the system.

Finally since the ear is not good at detecting vertical separation in sound sources the brain will narrow the gap between the cluster and the actor underneath and the effect of the system will be more authentic than with loudspeakers positioned at the sides of the stage. There is however some evidence that centre cluster systems need especial care in low-ceilinged rooms because the low-frequency beams are closer to the microphones below and hence push the system closer to feedback.

In traditional theatres loudspeakers are often found on either side of the proscenium and these positions are selected when some degree of stereo is required. However a stereo system is not ideal for vocal reinforcement because there are two sound paths to each audience member (one from each loudspeaker) and so not only might intelligibility suffer if the sounds arrive at substantially different times but also the two sound paths could contribute more reflections and

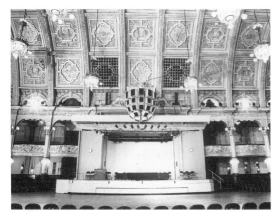

The Turbosound cluster installed at the Empress Ballroom Blackpool, favourite haunt of the Party Conferences.

Close up of the cluster showing the distribution of the loudspeakers.

push the system closer to feedback. Therefore stereo systems are more suited to sound effects work and to the amplification of orchestras. In this latter role the individually miked instruments are slightly panned so that their sound emerges relative to whichever loudspeaker is the nearer in

order that the aural and visual pictures match. Understandably a theatre system which comprises both stereo and centre cluster loudspeakers is very flexible and this is the format for many successful 'concert' systems in which the orchestral mix is fed to the stereo loudspeakers and the vocal mix to the centre cluster.

There is a variation on this in a system for which the author was the consultant at the Hexagon in Reading. In this multi-purpose venue a centre cluster was out of the question because it would have interfered with the lighting positions and so two clusters are used, thus offering a form of stereo. Arguably this format might become more familiar with the advent of infra-red stereo-imaging radio mics, these transmit to two receivers with the stronger signal going to the nearer receiver (and thence to the nearer loudspeaker) so that an actor's voice would move between the stereo loudspeakers as he moves around the stage.

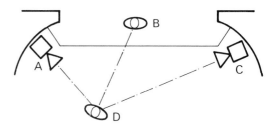

Ideally the speaker should be aimed as C so that the live sound BD comes from the same direction. There is confusion if the speaker is aimed as at A where the sound AD comes from the opposite direction to the live sound BD.

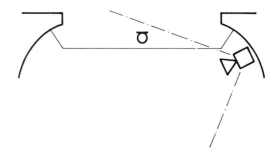

Care should be taken with aiming since some speakers have wide horizontal beams which can be picked up by the mic causing feedback.

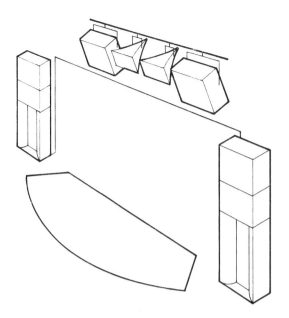

Simplified drawing of two separate systems. The stacks at the sides with bass bins, Mid range and HF horns are for stereo instrument reinforcement. The monitors and HF horns over the pros are for vocal reinforcement.

Quite often the centre cluster cannot adequately serve the area immediately underneath it in the front stalls and so small loudspeakers are placed by the proscenium to provide additional cover, these are known as 'side fills'. Another variation on this idea is to build several tiny loudspeakers into the front fascia of the stage or orchestra pit, as we saw earlier a 4" (0.10m) loudspeaker will deliver down to 100Hz so that such a system will lift the vocals for the front rows and support the cluster above. There is a similar problem with proscenium loudspeakers, especially if there are separate LF, mid and HF units. Unless all three systems are aimed down towards all the audience the front stalls will be light on mid and HF.

We have established above that in theatre systems where vocal reinforcement is the norm the fewer the number of loudspeaker groups then the clearer the sound will be and this leads the system design towards the centre cluster format. However in many auditoria the cluster cannot reach under the circle to the rear stalls, causing a sound shadow, and so this area has to be served

The sound system specified by the author for the Hexagon Reading showing the stereo Turbosound clusters.

by separate loudspeakers. The distance from the additional loudspeakers to the audience is far less than the distance from the actor to the same audience served by the additional loudspeakers and therefore there is a danger that the amplified sound will arrive before the direct live sound from the stage, confusing the brain and blurring the intelligibility. The answer is to electronically delay the amplified sound so that it arrives after the direct live sound, this way the brain seizes on the sound which arrives first and 'moves' other later sounds so that they appear to be coming from the same direction, this is known as the precedence effect discovered by Dr Haas as we saw earlier. A related problem occurs in large

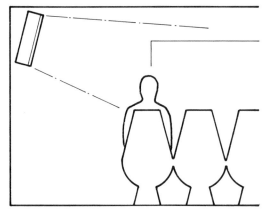

View from rear stalls to the stage showing how a speaker installed for the rear stalls blasts those nearest. Absorption would ensure that the centre stalls did not receive much level.

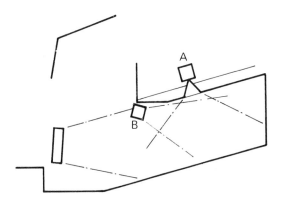

For the rear stalls' speakers hung from the ceiling A, or circle front B, are often the answer to this problem area. Delay lines would be necessary to maintain the directional effect and prevent overlapping sound paths from muddying the sound.

auditoria where stereo loudspeakers are employed at the sides of the proscenium, often these cannot effectively reach to the rear stalls and circle without losing both some high frequency content and sound pressure level caused by the grazing effect of the seats and the audience.

Therefore additional loudspeakers are positioned mid-auditorium on each level but again these are nearer to the rear audience than the proscenium loudspeakers and if the difference in sound paths is more than 40' (about 12m and measured at 14°C) then the intelligibility will suffer in these areas. Again the answer is to apply a delay to the mid auditorium chain so that their sound arrives after the proscenium chain. The sound pressure level of the delayed loudspeaker is important because it relates to the brain's ability to detect that loudspeaker as a separate source.

In order for the precedence effect to work some increase in SPL of the delayed system above the main system or live sound is essential. Below 6dB difference the delayed loudspeaker will be undetectable (and many people believe such systems are not working!) but at 10dB difference the delayed loudspeaker is clearly audible.

ARTICULATION LOSS

The function of a sound system is to transmit information and if we concern ourselves with the transmission of verbal information, where much of the clarity is contained in the consonants, then we can state that a successful system is one that loses only a small proportion of consonants. Early telephone and recording engineers were interested in discovering what percentage of consonants could be lost before the content became unintelligible. They found that if less than 10% of consonants are lost then the intelligibility will be very good and between 10% and 15% the intelligibility will only be acceptable if the vocal projection is good but that if progressively more than 15% of consonants are lost then the intelligibility will be poor, 15% is therefore taken as the limit.

The success of the intelligibility depends

essentially on two factors (ignoring if we can the vocal projection of the actor). These are the ability of the loudspeaker to deliver its information to the desired area and the influence of the sound which reverberates around the room on the direct amplified sound. Clearly a successful system is one where the loudspeakers are directional and the reverberation is low and in most theatres these two criteria can be easily met and therefore in these situations the following calculations are not necessary. However in large arenas and other places where the acoustics are difficult (such as churches and swimming pools), the distances are so vast that the benefits of directional systems are harder to maintain and the reverberation time is longer blurring the words. Therefore in difficult areas it is vital to be able to predict how successful a given system will be and conversely how to design a system in order to achieve a certain measure of success. In 1971 as a result of experiments in Holland the following formula was produced for this purpose:

$$\% \ Alcons = \frac{200(D2)^2 \times (Rt60)^2 \times (n+1)}{Volume \times Q \ of \ loudspeakers \times M}$$

where **% Alcons** is the percentage of lost consonants

D2 is the distance from the loudspeaker to the furthest audience member

Rt60 is the Reverberation Time

n is the number of loudspeaker groups

V is the volume on cubic meters

M is usually 1, although in fact it can be used in its more accurate form where it is the product of M = (1 − average absorption coefficient in the room) × (1 − absorption in area covered by the loudspeaker).

*all measurements are metric, if imperial is used change the 200 constant to 641.81. Before we use the equations let us look more closely at the terms Q and n.

Q OF LOUDSPEAKERS

The Q of a loudspeaker is the ratio of its horizontal beam angle to its vertical beam angle, where the beam angles are measured at a sound pres-

sure level 6dB down of that on axis. It therefore follows that a loudspeaker with very wide beam angles will have a low Q whereas a loudspeaker with narrow beam angles will have a high Q. Here are typical values for different designs of loudspeaker:

mid/low frequency unit − 180° horizontal/ 180° vertical × Q is 2
line source column − 180° horizontal/40° vertical × Q is 9
HF horn − 40° horizontal/40° vertical × Q is 26°

The higher the Q of a loudspeaker then the better it will contain its information within the desired area and not add that information to the reverberant room. Furthermore the higher the Q of a loudspeaker then the higher the sound pressure level will be on its axis, for every doubling of Q the on-axis SPL increases by 3dB, hence from the above figures. 180° × 180° is a hemisphere which has a Q of 2 and a SPL 1 of +3dB; 180° × 90° will have a Q of 4 and +3dB to the SPL 1; 180° × 45° will have a Q of 8 and +6dB to the SPL 1. The formula for calculating Q is as follows:

$$Q = \frac{180°}{arc \ sin \left(\frac{sin \ horizontal \ angle}{2} \times \frac{sin \ vertical \ angle}{2} \right)}$$

NUMBER OF LOUDSPEAKER GROUPS n

The more separate loudspeaker groups there are then the higher will be the reverberant sound in the auditorium and hence the consonants will be in danger of being obscured. The fewer the number of loudspeakers then the less they will contribute to the reverberant field and hence it will be easier to achieve a good separation between the direct sound level and the reverberant sound level. This is essentially the principle behind the centre cluster as we saw earlier and although several actual loudspeakers are contained within the cluster itself, the structure as a whole represents one loudspeaker group.

USING THE FORMULA

When designing a sound system for an existing building the distances, volume and reverberation time will be known, or at least they can be calculated. Therefore the missing factor here is the Q of the loudspeaker and this can be found by re-arranging the formula as below with the % Alcons being held at the minimum 15% level:

$$\text{minimum } Q \text{ for 15\% Alcons} = \frac{200(D2)^2 \times (Rt60)^2 \times (n+1)}{15 \times volume \times M}$$

where **D2** is the distance from the loudspeaker to the furthest audience member

Rt60 is the reverberation time

n is the number of loudspeaker groups

M is 1 in most cases (see above)

Q is the directivity ratio of the loudspeaker

In a new building there could be some influence on its design exerted by the needs of the sound system in terms of the maximum distance that the audience could be from the loudspeakers and in terms of the maximum reverberation time for an articulation loss of 15%. The formulae are at the foot of the page.

There are some general guidelines when using these equations:

a) Aim for a separation between the direct amplified sound and the reverberant, back-ground sound of 25dB. This can be reduced to 10dB if the reverberation time is very short (say 0.5 sec) as it might be in a small auditorium.

b) It is easier (and cheaper) to increase the Q of the loudspeaker/s than to lower the rever-beration time if the reverberant field is too strong.

c) The values of Q are limited by loudspeaker design and by how the individual loudspeakers are mounted together.

For example we have seen from the above that the values range from a single LF/mid unit at 2

(and which would require an additional HF unit) to 9 for a column and 26 for a horn. Few HF units have values higher than 26 although there are some HF horns with a 40° horizontal × 20° vertical pattern which produces a Q of 51. Else-where Q values higher than 26 (40° × 40° hori-zontal × vertical pattern) can only be achieved by stacking the horns in line source format.

In theory each additional horn reduces the vertical beam angle by 50% and therefore two 40° × 40° horns would produce a Q of 52. In reality the vertical beam angle of stacked horns is reduced by about one third and therefore there would be a correspondingly smaller increase in Q. Many designers are reluctant to use horns in such narrow (long throw) configurations because they feel the design introduces coloura-tion to the HF sound.

The distance from the loudspeakers at which the level of the sound system and the level of the reverberant sound in the room are equal is known as the Critical Distance and the formula for calculating Dc is as follows:

$$Dc = 0.03121 \sqrt{\frac{Q \text{ (from above)} \times Volume \times M \text{ (1 } - constant)}{Rt60 \times (n+1)}}$$

As the Q increases (and consequently the number of loudspeaker groups can be decreased) then the Critical Distance can be increased, in fact every quadrupling of Q doubles the Critical Distance, hence the more directional the loudspeaker then the further away the sound will be intelligible in a reverberant room although beyond an Rt of 1.6 seconds no-one should be more than 3.16 times the Critical Distance away from the loudspeakers. The distance between the microphone and the loudspeaker should ideally be more than the Critical Distance if feed-back is to be avoided.

$$\text{maximum distance of audience to loudspeaker, metres} = \sqrt{\frac{15 \times volume \times Q \times M}{200 \ (Rt60)^2 \times (n+1)}}$$

$$\text{maximum Rt60 for 15\% Alcons} = \sqrt{\frac{15 \times volume \times Q \times M}{200 \times (D2)^2 \times (n+1)}}$$

The following example of the use of the above formulae illustrates just how valuable the calculations can be when difficult acoustics are encountered.

The author was asked to design an audio visual installation for an historical exhibit, housed in a disused courtroom. The building was listed and so alterations of any kind were not permitted and indeed would have interfered with the authenticity of the exhibit. The design brief was to create a sense of courtroom proceedings by playing recorded voices through loud-speakers concealed around the courtroom itself and supported by simultaneous projections and models. In all there were to be seven locations.

The room was comparatively small, 42' (13m) square and with a volume of 28,800 cubic feet (815 cubic metres). However because there were almost no absorbent surfaces in the courtroom at all, the Rt60 at 500Hz was 2.5 seconds. This altered little when the absorption of the 'audience' (under 90 people) was added to the

calculation, and in any case the system was required to perform to standard when only a small number of people were present, so the effect of the audience was ignored in the calculations.

Such a reverberant acoustic is not favourable for speech and it compares poorly with the kind of Rt one would expect in a conventional theatre (at the same volume the Rt in that situation would be less than 1 second at 500Hz). The difficulty therefore was to design a system in which the Articulation Loss would be less than 15% when several loudspeakers would be in use simultaneously and from different parts of the court, thus adding to the overall reverberant sound.

The first stage was to identify a range of loudspeakers which were broadly suitable and capable of being hidden easily; three types were chosen. Then, using the manufacturers' data of horizontal and vertical beam angles, the Q of each loudspeaker was calculated from the above

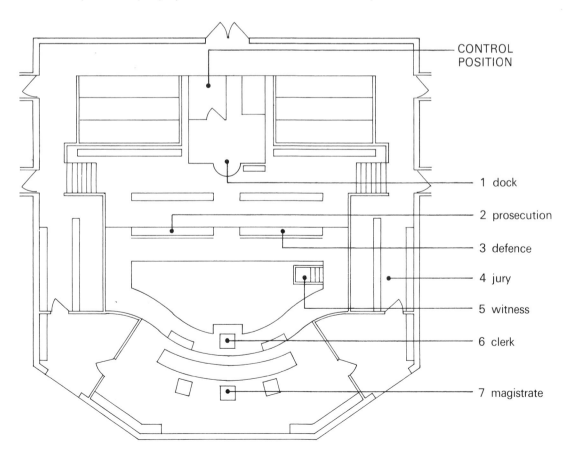

CONTROL
POSITION

1 dock

2 prosecution

3 defence

4 jury

5 witness

6 clerk

7 magistrate

Loudspeaker Beam at 6dB down point, Horizontal × Vertical beam angles	Number of speakers live at one time	Distance of speakers to audience		Articulation lost
	N –	D2 –	Q –	%
Version one – centre cluster only				
1A – 100° × 100°	1	18′ (5.49m)	5	18.05%
1B – 180° × 60°	1	"	6	15.05%
1C – 90° × 40°	1	"	12	7.52%
Version two – distributed system all on simultaneously				
2A – 100° × 100°	7	10′ (3.05m)	5	22.28%
2B – 180° × 60°	7	"	6	18.57%
2C – 90° × 40°	7	"	12	9.28%
Version three – distributed system – selected loudspeakers				
3A – 100° × 100°	3	10′ (3.05m)	5	13.92%
3B – 180° × 60°	3	"	6	11.60%
3C – 90° × 40°	3	"	12	5.80%

formula. Then the data was fed into the Articulation Loss calculations in order to assess what overall clarity was obtained from the different formats. In version one the design was based on a centre cluster format suspended above the court, which it was thought might be useful for general commentary. Version two illustrates the same general commentary idea but this time via all seven distributed loudspeakers hidden in the court and with no centre cluster. Finally version three illustrates the same idea but using only 3 of the above selected loudspeakers simultaneously for added clarity.

The table above was obtained.

Version one is interesting in that it produces the (not very surprising) statistic that only the high Q 90° × 40° device (1C) will deliver safely under the 15% limit and therefore this is the only loudspeaker useful for the centre cluster. However the audience was not stationary in one defined area and so the area covered by the cluster would require a much wider beam angle, and this could be achieved by adding more loudspeakers of the same type. However the cluster is comparatively obtrusive and therefore version two attempts to

discover what the articulation loss would be if all the concealed loudspeakers were used simultaneously without any cluster. As before only the 90° × 40° device (2C) is acceptable. However with such a pattern of narrow horizontal beam angles it is possible that odd waveforms could be set up creating areas of emphasis or sharp cut off in the sound as people move around.

In version three any of the loudspeakers are acceptable because they each produce less than a 15% loss of articulation. The success of this format is clearly related to the number of loudspeakers live simultaneously and so three was the maximum operating parameter. In terms of loudspeaker type, in version three, loudspeaker no 2 produces the best overall performance in that its beam offers the best dispersion horizontally without spreading too far vertically and the percentage articulation loss still permits some error to be made before the 15% limit is reached.

In the above example, the Rt and the volume already existed and could not be changed (the most common situation), and therefore it was the other parameters, the Q of the loudspeakers and the number live at one time, which were the variables.

Finally loudspeakers are the most prominent visual section of the sound system and so their location and colour must be discussed with the architect. Regrettably some loudspeakers are rejected because they are considered to be too large and so the system suffers for the sake of appearances. Fortunately loudspeakers are becoming smaller as computers help with their design. Architects tend to want to hide loudspeakers or position them away from focal points in the building and system designers often have to educate planners that loudspeaker positions are not unimportant.

All loudspeakers can easily be painted at little extra cost and even the largest unit takes on a more pleasant aspect when it matches the decor. Speaker cloth colour is more difficult since it is usually available only in large quantity, and alteration from a manufacturer's standard can be expensive. It is worth discussing alternative materials with the manufacturer, some conventional cloths or expanded metal grilles are acceptable if they do not impede the high frequency response. In new buildings it is often possible to construct slots in walls and ceilings which are large enough for speaker manoeuvres, and which are covered with speaker cloth so that the slot opening is unobtrusive. Suspended cluster systems require structural work and access for maintenance and it is sensible to locate these close to a catwalk or to provide a hoist.

So far we have been examining the equipment and its application primarily as it relates to proscenium theatres and halls. Now let us look at other venues.

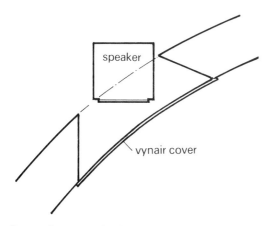

Concealing a speaker in a wall void.

THEATRE IN THE ROUND AND THRUST STAGES

Firstly, let us establish the shapes that we have in mind with respect to these two terms. The term theatre-in-the-round (often abbreviated to TIR) applies where the performing area is central and surrounded by the audience; the term thrust applies where the audience are only on three sides of the stage.

The Royal Exchange, Manchester.

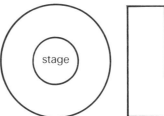

Theatre in the round, audience on all sides.

Thrust stage, audience on three sides.

Now let us consider the scale of the problems. In small auditoria, typically many TIR venues, the intelligibility contour created by the performer will be likely to encompass all the seats, even those behind him, and it can be no accident that some of the most successful theatres of this type have been modest in size.

By comparison, thrust auditoria can be quite large, because they often resemble indoor Greek ampitheatres, the most famous examples being at Stratford Ontario and Chichester in England. In buildings of this type the large auditorium creates problems since some people will be outside the intelligibility contour and will therefore not hear clearly, and of course the situation is exacerbated by poor projection from the actors. There is some evidence that large auditoria of this type have occasionally utilised discrete sound reinforcement, but the subject is usually a sore point and questions are not popular.

A small theatre in the round needing no reinforcement of the voice since all seats are within the intelligibility contour.

Because the performing area is now located in the auditorium, the two main problems are avoidance of feedback and maintenance of directability. Feedback can be minimised by using the techniques we have already discussed – directional mics and loudspeakers, and room equalisation.

Where discrete reinforcement is paramount, loudspeaker positioning is critical but in these shapes there is no proscenium wall on which to mount loudspeakers, the back wall of the thrust stage being too far back for correct directability and because it is behind the mics, loudspeakers in this position could push the system closer to feedback. The only possible location is over the stage itself with the simplest loudspeaker installation being a centre cluster with a wide horizontal beam angle and a relatively narrow vertical beam angle. This suggests that the cluster should include horns for the HF and should also taper the response of the LF in order to avoid feedback which would most certainly occur if high sound levels are involved and if the stage is large so that the mics would be in front of the cluster. Some

situations require a more distributed loudspeaker system with the loudspeakers hung closer to the edge of the stage and where the beam is less likely to be looking directly into float microphones.

Often these systems can be designed to provide greater directional authenticity (than would be possible on a large stage from a centre cluster) because some degree of stereo imaging is possible for each bank of seats. This is achieved by mixing float mics with a predominence to the nearest loudspeaker above and then at a slightly lower level to all other loudspeakers serving the other seats. As a result of this technique, mixers for TIR work tend to be sophisticated possessing more outputs (at least two per bank of seats) than might be the case with a mixer assigned to a proscenium production. Furthermore the above systems are assumed to be provided for either discrete vocal reinforcement or direct amplification on musicals, once sound effects are also considered, with loudspeakers distributed behind and over the audience, the mixer needs many outputs, often as many as the number of inputs, and it is no accident that the first computer assisted mixers were conceived in this situation.

Since there are so many outputs, equalisation of room acoustics is expensive, but this is the only way of levelling out the peaks and troughs and providing more gain before feedback. Musicals also require foldback to artists on stage and these are also best placed overhead with the other loudspeakers, but feedback is likely and sundry measures have to be taken; to overcome this problem the author has often used frequency shifters and these have given just the extra bit of level required. The author successfully used frequency shifters with horn loudspeakers in his design for an overhead foldback system at the 'Talk of the Town' theatre restaurant in London, conventional wedges would have been too obtrusive and since the performers' mics were pointing up into the horns, feedback was more likely.

The design principles above form the basis for large arena systems although because these venues tend to be reverberant it is sensible to cut down the power of the centre speaker array in favour of a second or even a third circle of loudspeakers working to time delay. Unless the loud-speakers could be kept very directional it is wiser to opt for several delayed loudspeakers producing a low level rather than a few loudspeakers producing a lot of level which could indiscriminately bounce around the room damaging the last syllables. It should be appreciated that the delay is provided to prevent several sound paths from overlapping and 'muddying' the sound, rather than to preserve the directional effect which in large venues sometimes has to take second place to clarity. The articulation loss equations can be especially useful in large arena systems.

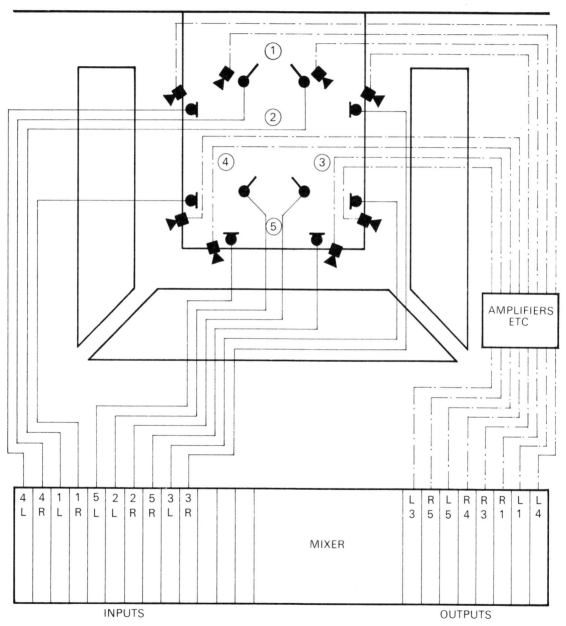

Simplified drawing of a system for reinforcement of a thrust stage. Each mic is fed to a speaker serving its own area but is also fed at a lower level to all other speakers.

One of the main problems with these areas is that speakers need to be in view, and this upsets architects. It is important to explain why a loudspeaker position is unavoidable and to work together on some shape for the rig and colour that is the least objectionable. It is especially important to overcome the view that good sound is impossible in large venues so loudspeaker positions do not matter. Indeed in the realms of large venues with poor acoustics, good positions are as vital as ever.

Today, large venues are the only location for expensive stars who need vast audiences to support high expenses. Conversely, big stars may appear live so seldom that vast audiences are likely. Concerts can take place in areas previously unconsidered as locations for music, with consequent acoustic problems. In these cases it is vital that the planners all get together – and that includes those responsible for the seating layout, since the acoustician may deem it necessary to drape walls or voids to cut down reverberation, and loudspeakers may need some extra overhead support. Finally production schedules must be planned to accommodate long fit ups and allow the balancing of sound systems when others are not working.

In general terms, high-quality high-level sound systems are too expensive for any large venue to consider their purchase as a permanent feature, systems toured by popular groups for

A rock system (a small one!) comprising bass bins, mid units and HF horns, some rock musicians play in front of systems like this, each musician serving the part of the stack behind him.

such areas frequently cost well over £500,000. The problem is the requirement of both large quantities of loudspeakers and amplifiers, and of expensive and complex delay and equalisation backup. Therefore for short term use it is more cost-effective to rent from the many specialised companies now in existence, and a by-product of this method is that expertise is also available.

TOURING

Because the provision of good equipment by theatres is patchy (for a variety of reasons but mostly economics) it is often preferable for companies to tour their own system. This also overcomes compatibility problems with alien plugs and sockets and ensures some consistency in sound effects and mixing levels since the same operator is working with the same system throughout the life of the show.

The obvious requirement of equipment going on tour is that it should be robust and capable of withstanding the most violent handling. Crews are often not respectful of the equipment being removed from a theatre in pouring rain at two o'clock in the morning. The most sensible provision is that of the 'flight' case – an aluminium box lined with foam rubber cut to the shape of the equipment it holds. Wheels and handles on such boxes not only make life easier for the crew but can prevent mishandling.

Plugs and cables come in for the most misuse, and spare parts, including spare made-up cables to save time, are essential as well as a well-equipped tool kit. Equipment is now available to test cables and connectors in order to locate faults quickly, but patience on the get-out when uncoiling and unplugging is the best protection.

On no account should any venue come as a surprise, a prior visit is vital to check mains supplies, connectors and locations; house sound systems (as back up and for background house music); house electrical staff; local service source; and acoustics. It is especially useful to seek the opinions of local staff on dead spots and other acoustic problems, five minutes' chat can save hours of experimenting.

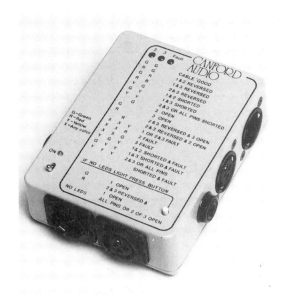

A cable testing device from Canford Audio for long and short runs, balanced and unbalanced lines.

Above all it is vital that there is time to set up the system properly, if there is not time to do this there is little point in touring a system, since the result would be unlikely to justify the effort and expense involved. Of course as we saw earlier the development of auto-tuning graphic equalisers means that a group could quickly tune any system to the acoustic of their choice.

One thorny problem is that of the location of the sound mixing desk. We have seen that it is desirable for this to be located in the auditorium, but in some venues this can come as a shock to managements, especially when accompanied with untidy cabling. Prior discussion on this is vital, both to prevent the sale of relevant seats and to work out cable runs that won't upset the manager or the local safety officer. Many new buildings are fitted with ducting and cable hooks so that visitors' cable can be easily and discretely installed. Visitors will use these facilities if they are in the correct location, and a survey of visitors' choices will help to obtain this information. We have also seen that all systems require to be fed by current-balance earth-leakage circuit-breakers. Electrical installations, maintenance and regulations vary widely and these devices are essential for ensuring safety.

It is an especially good idea to keep an index of venues used with both data and comments in preparation for the next visit. On no account should such details be confined to one person's memory.

SWIMMING POOLS AND CHURCHES

Although we are primarily concerned with entertainment sound, which suggests theatre buildings, sufficient activity is taking place in sports and religious buildings to warrant our attention. Essentially, they have one common problem – long reverberation times which prolong the last syllable in each word and obscures all but the slowest speech (this is one reason that church services contain long, slow syllable phrasing).

In these areas, it is a mistake to introduce high sound levels from a small number of loudspeakers unless the loudspeakers are exceptionally directional. The only answer is to provide as many loudspeakers as possible and keep the sound level very, very low. Ideally no one should be far from a loudspeaker and this does of course suggest that the directional effect has to be sacrificed although in churches some realism can be maintained by providing delay lines relative to the pulpit and the lectern mic positions.

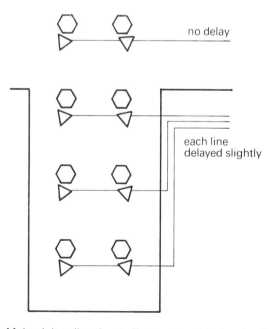

Maintaining directional effect in church by low level units each pair with its own delay line.

In churches we would usually be dealing with speech-only systems and voice reinforcement level rather than high level amplification. There is therefore some justification for the argument in favour of using restricted frequency systems to prevent much low frequency sound from reverberating around the building. The response of a BBC-designed column for such locations is a useful guide at 100Hz – 8kHz. A graphic equaliser is also especially valuable in such systems since standing waves can create havoc with feedback and frequency corrections are necessary. The voice can also be given some 'attack' in this way since the mixer in these cases is likely to be simpler than those found in theatres and lack extensive equalisation.

Directional microphones are essential to prevent the pickup of background noise and cut down feedback, and directional loudspeakers are also required which would normally (but not exclusively) mean columns. There are several small 'speech only' columns on the market which should not be used in these situations since their reduced size prevents the beam from being very directional – the longer the column the more directional it will be (some professional church reinforcement systems use loudspeakers 10' long). Some work has been carried out in the U.S.A. with horn loudspeaker systems in churches and swimming pools and with some success, especially in the former where the buildings are designed more on the arena principle than the conventional crucifix. The centre cluster method can be applied to churches but generally only in modern buildings where the cluster location can be concealed, in any event the cluster will need extensive low frequency cut-off probably below 150Hz.

In both swimming pools and churches the articulation loss equation mentioned earlier will prove especially helpful since the volume, reverberation time and desired articulation loss will be known and therefore the equations can be used to determine the number of loudspeakers, their ideal Q and distance to the furthest audience member.

In the case of new buildings, or those being refurbished it is evident that it is easier to apply absorbent acoustic treatment to swimming pools rather than to traditional churches although perhaps in time churches will benefit from the antiphase reverberation time system mentioned earlier in the book.

BANQUETS

Banquets take place in a variety of settings, in a low ceiling room – a restaurant, exhibition gallery, theatre or foyer.

In these events the location of the top table – the presumed location of the speechmaker – is paramount. It is especially useful if this can be located on a raised platform – perhaps on stage if it is not required for a dance band or cabaret. A good sightline will help acoustics and the reception of the speech.

Small wide range loudspeaker on stand ideal for banquet work.

If there is a sound system installed in the room it is often facing the wrong way for any kind of authenticity (and likely to feedback when the mic is turned up!) and whilst this may appear a detail, many a speech has been hampered by the sound creeping up behind the audience. In general it is best to avoid the house system and provide good portable speakers on stands in the body of the hall itself. These can thus be positioned to help the directional effect, reduce feedback, and angled to avoid reflections and standing waves.

Since most speechmakers need to address people over a wide angle it is desirable to provide two microphones to cover all the arc of speech. In this case the polarity – the way in which each mic is wired – needs careful checking, since opposing wiring will cause signal cancellations. PCC or PZM mics are useful when mounted on lecterns since they will allow a wide arc of movement for the speechmaker and should be almost invisible on the lectern.

Banquets are frequently accompanied by cabaret or disco and it is wiser to accept that each function must have its own system. This may mean untidy cables, but does not put all the eggs in one basket, and ensures all relevant criteria are met. A speech system is not a disco system is not a cabaret system.

LOW CEILINGS

If we consider the normal approach to sound system design applied to a room with a low ceiling, we find that the loudspeaker beam cannot reach to the rear of the room without absorption by those seated nearby.

We have mentioned earlier that in the church a

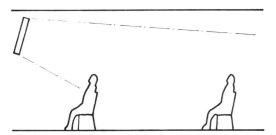

Line source columns cannot easily reach the rear rows in low rooms because of the grazing effect.

small column speaker, which might be considered a solution to this problem, would not act as a full column in radiating sound (nor would it be likely to have a good frequency response for multipurpose use). The only answer therefore is to mount a number of single drivers, perhaps concealed in the ceiling itself. An 8" (0.20m) diameter driver provides quite an acceptable sound in a very small ceiling space although it would be sensible to provide wider range units if the budget permits. Where there is no ceiling cavity it is worth considering surface mounting small cabinet units under the ceiling rather than on the walls. If a centre cluster is considered we have mentioned before that centre cluster systems need especial care in low ceiling rooms because of the proximity of the low frequency beams to the microphones which might push the system closer to feedback.

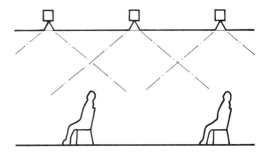

Overhead speakers in a low ceiling room provide an even distribution of sound; a directional effect can be maintained by introducing delay lines for each row of speakers; the speaker beams should intersect at ear level.

In all cases it is vital to achieve a good, even coverage of sound – the directional effect being secondary – and a section of the room should be drawn in order to calculate the correct beam dispersion which should aim to have the loudspeaker beams intersecting at ear level. We stated earlier that the consonants are contained within the 150–4000Hz band and it is the loudspeaker's beam in these frequencies that should be drawn, allowing also for some overlap. In a large, low ceiling area, the difference in multiple sound paths might be such that time delay systems are needed to restore clarity, a similarity with the large arena described above. Remember that a difference of more than 40' (13m) in sound paths produces a distinct echo and therefore a delay would be needed on each line of loudspeakers away from the main platform.

In some cases rooms cannot have one fixed focal point. This creates two problems; firstly the likelihood of a mic being positioned under a loudspeaker and thus generating feedback, and secondly the time-delay network is worthless unless altered each time the focal point of the room shifts. The first problem is easier to solve by simply switching off the loudspeaker closest to the mic, and therefore in flexible rooms each loudspeaker must be separately wired back to a switch or patch panel. The second problem is more complex although solvable if the different locations of focus (hence the relationship of sound paths) are predictable and repeated because once the delay setting and gain setting is known for each format it can be recreated each time using the digital delay unit's memory facility.

OUTDOOR SYSTEMS

We have seen that the shape and treatment of surfaces in a room can create good or bad acoustics leading to reverberation times which are a help or a hindrance. But in outdoor events there are no reflections and the reverberation time is nil. Outdoors the air is the only tool at the designer's disposal and it is important that the effects of wind and temperature are understood.

It is often said that sound carries when the wind is blowing towards the listener. This is an erroneous assumption. What actually happens when the wind and sound are travelling in the same direction is that the wind cools the lower levels of air causing the sound waves to be refracted towards the listener. Wind blowing against the sound causes sound waves to be refracted upwards and away from the listener. Therefore loudspeakers for open air events should always be pointing with the prevailing wind to cover the largest area or against the wind to restrict coverage to a small area.

Another important aspect is that of the necessary sound pressure level. We have seen earlier that this must be more than the level of the ambient noise, and that a headroom of 25dB is

Helping those outdoors to see and hear better, a stand at Hidcote Manor.

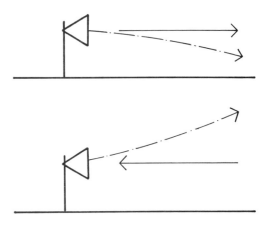

Outdoor speaker location; with the wind for the sound to cover a large distance, against the wind for the sound to cover a small distance. The effect is due to the refraction of the air caused by the cooling of the wind.

sensible if people are to hear clearly without fatigue. Because outdoor events frequently generate 70dB background noise, allowing for our desired 25dB headroom, the inverse square law dictates that a loudspeaker producing 110dB at 4' with full power could be heard 16' (5m) away before the background level of 70dB became dangerous. This would suggest that a large number of loudspeakers would be needed. Of course if the background level was lower, say at 60dB and we lowered our headroom to 10dB then the same loudspeaker could cover a distance of over 250' and hence fewer would be needed. These considerations obviously also need to take into account the horizontal dispersion of the loudspeaker in the speech frequency range (150–4000Hz) and templates can be placed on maps to check coverage. Elevating the loudspeakers on towers, truck or buildings reduces the grazing effect and lessening the effects of the inverse square law.

It is especially important that the loudspeakers relate to the movement and direction that the audience are facing; they must face the same way or else wind movements and time delays induced by distances can create disturbing echoes. In this respect some time delay might also be useful to prevent seriously overlapping beams from muddying the sound.

Where there is some structure, either natural or man-made, it is important to use it as a supportive reflecting surface by focusing the sound away from the surface and not towards it – a process that would create reflections. There is good evidence to suggest that some of the greatest outdoor orations were set against natural cliffs and early Greek theatre orchestras were set against a reflective wall. Indeed the Greeks were very skilled at outdoor acoustics, using the natural slope of ground wherever possible to create the seating banks.

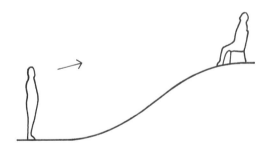

Location of audience outdoors, use natural structures like hills as a seating tier and let the land fall away to a natural focal point.

Equipment outdoors must obviously be weatherproof and this suggests the metal horn speaker in preference to the flimsier moving coil types. Good quality horns are available in speech frequencies and they might come as a surprise to some listeners' usual expectation of thin, tinny public address normally associated with outdoor events. As with most pieces of sound equipment – good units are not cheap. The choice, and use, of microphone is also important. It still has to be cardioid even though there is no reverberant

acoustic and little chance of feedback. There is however much background noise that we do not want picked up. Mics should always have some wind filter fitted, and are frequently used too close to the mouth and with too much level so that distortion results. It is vital that the excitement of the moment is conveyed without shouting. There are some close-talk commentator's mics available (also known as lip mics) and these are preferable to ordinary cardioids.

Outdoor events are, by their nature, temporary and great care is needed in rigging and connecting. It is wise to ensure spares are available and not to run one circuit of speakers round the ground from one amplifier. Several circuits from several amps might be more expensive but it is more flexible, easier to balance and safer. Constant voltage systems will be the more usual because the cable lengths will be considerable and low-impedance systems would suffer much signal loss.

OPERATING

The 'black boxes' that form a sound system frequently appear to have a life of their own; inhabited by a (silent) spirit which withholds its secrets and often refuses to cooperate at embarrassing moments. Even experienced engineers display a certain amount of relief when a reasonable sound emerges on the first occasion of a system's use! Sound equipment must never be taken for granted but treated with respect at all times and by all people.

The design of sound in the theatre is in its infancy by comparison with the other technical departments of costumes, scenery and lighting. We are accustomed to the realisation of sets, costumes and lighting involving a high degree of both creativity and considerable technical support. By comparison, sound appears to be a technical response to a technical problem, there appears to be almost no creative aspect and in both England and the United States only a mere handful of individuals are well known for their artistic interpretation of the reinforcement of voice and the generation of sound effects. Perhaps this is because the medium is intangible and subjective to a high degree. But it must also

The sophisticated mixing desk at the Royal Opera House.

be because the funds have consistently been denied this branch of theatre, so the dreams of many must remain largely dreams. Another reason is the reluctance of managements to permit sound system designers to locate their equipment in the most appropriate part of the theatre. However there are signs that these problems are being overcome, notably on the big West End or Broadway productions which so often introduce new techniques.

Of course it is possible to become more concerned about the hardware than about the sound itself. Just as a lighting designer must think in terms of pictures rather than of instruments, then so must the sound system designer imagine the level and quality that he wants to hear from the system before he becomes bogged down in knobs and decibels. He must visit the theatre and try to put himself in the audience's place, imagining the relationship of the direct sounds of the actors' voices and the orchestra blending with those sounds coming from his sound system.

The most frequent criticism levelled at designers is that their systems generate too much volume. An analysis of such comments can reveal a variety of unsupported claims, adjacent couples often argue, one felt the level was good, the other too loud, whose opinion does the designer listen to? Occasionally the patron disliked the other aspects of the show but found sound the easiest target for his criticism. However spurious, all such complaints should be logged on a seating plan which should also indicate other contributary factors, such as who was operating the mixer at the time. Eventually, if there is a genuine problem then it will emerge on the plan and appropriate action can be taken; the seating plan should be marked in front of the patron who will feel comforted that he has been listened to.

A key person in any debate about sound levels is obviously the operator himself and a good designer has to consider this individual as a part of his overall scheme and hence he must be brought into the design stage. Sadly all too frequently the sound operator is the assistant stage manager who doesn't have many props that week, but the operator must appreciate what the designer is trying to achieve, levels he is aiming for and why, sound systems do not always have to be pushed to their limits merely because more level is available!

Above all the operator must listen. This is very difficult because by the time that the show is run in he will know the script very well. This means that he may subconsciously think the sound is clear, but this is actually because he knows the words and his brain is providng the missing links from its memory bank. Hence he may not make the adjustments that are needed.

There can be no doubt that in order to hear properly the operator must be in the same acoustic as his audience (if this means that someone else has to do props then so be it). Access to the same acoustic by means of a removable control room window is not quite the same thing as sitting in the rear stalls because not only might the control room not be in a direct line to the loudspeakers but the width of the window might prevent some wavelengths from successfully reaching the operator.

Although the equalisation on the mixer might be set by the designer in rehearsal the operator should not merely be regarded as someone to operate effects and push channels faders up and down. The operator must understand all the controls in front of him so that he can make adjustments whilst the designer is away and when the atmosphere and the actors' voices are changing.

More specifically the operator should take note of the following:

1. Ensure the mixer area has a good plot space and sufficient low level light sources to illuminate all the controls without dazzling the audience nearby.

2. Before setting levels check to see if all relevant air-handling plant is switched on, the author knows of a system that produces 66dB in the rear stalls!

3. Switch on the amplifiers last (and switch them off first) ... (don't look for faulty connections with the channel faders up).

4. Don't inherit someone else's mixer settings, reset the whole desk to zero or centre before starting.

5. Always listen to levels in the positions farthest from the stage first and listen to each section of the theatre before putting all the system on together. Remember the ambient level is higher in the middle of the theatre because of audience noise.

6. Set the input gains to the lowest position and then push the channel, group and master faders to full. Turn the input gains up till the mic/s ring and then just back.

Use the faders with some gain in hand, that is with the faders back from full by 5, 10 or 15dB.

Always use lower levels in rehearsal and keep some in hand for the show when musicians play louder and drown the vocalist! (The audience will also absorb sound.)

7. Set the equalisation gently, often only minor adjustments are needed, more would generate a peak which would push the system closer to feedback. Emphasise the middle frequencies on vocals for greater attack.

Remember that a clear system doesn't have to be loud.

8. Remember that everytime the number of microphones in use doubles that the system goes 3dB closer to feedback so always use the minimum number of mics at one time.

BUDGETS, TENDERS AND SPECIFICATIONS

Finally of course it comes down to money and the budget is surely the most important aspect of any installation; yet so many times does the manager estimate a figure at one in the morning when professional advice is denied him. Since Local Authorities are obliged to consider most seriously the lowest tender, almost irrespective of its performance, the whole system is flawed from the start. How can any manager be expected, unaided, to realistically estimate the cost of a new system when most are replaced on average every ten years, a period of two generations in electronics terms and during which fundamental design changes will have taken place in equipment and systems.

Managers do rely on suppliers for advice but, apart from their obvious commercial interest, suppliers are often asked to quote without any technical specification being available or without having any idea of the budget and hence their advice is flawed. Of course if the budget figure is known, without expert advice the manager is often unable to judge which supplier's system is likely to be the best. A similar problem occurs if individual prices are given, because this tempts people to compare individual items of equipment even though they are actually buying a whole system. One way around this is to ask for separate envelopes for the price and performance data; the price envelopes are opened first and only those suppliers whose figures are appropriate are awarded the opening of the performance envelope.

Ideally good advice should be sought from independent consultants who can assess the problems, create a design brief and advise on which tender is the most suitable. Sound systems today cost a lot of money, are installed for many years and form a vital part of the presentation of the venue's product, under those circumstances it is foolish not to take independant advice. Sadly specifications created by house engineers are frequently centred around a limited knowledge of fashionable brand names and the consequent presumption that those items will make a system and achieve a defined performance is frequently false. Furthermore the items will probably be a personal choice which is often unpopular with the person's successor. Only a specification of the performance of the system will ensure that the client's needs are met. However performance specifications are unpopular with some suppliers simply because they are unable to understand acoustics and are frequently unaware of the performance characteristics of their own equipment. Consequently performance specifications tend to automatically return the better suppliers and deter the others.

The consultant and eventual tenderers need to know what the system is expected to do and there are several requirements each of which might suggest different equipment:

a) discrete voice reinforcement
b) amplification for musicals etc
c) rock sound, group systems etc
d) sound effects
e) all or any of these combined!

In all cases the specification also needs to set out the following aspects:

a) performance criteria
b) appearance criteria (of loudspeakers)
c) restrictions on locations of loudspeakers and mixer
d) schedule of spares required
e) request for service and emergency call-out data
f) supplier's other installations
g) supplier's references from past installations
h) availability times of the site
i) training and system handbook requirements
j) responsibilities, damages etc.

One of the most crucial aspects of the performance criteria is the target sound pressure level (together with an indication of what headroom is also needed). If asked most operators will opt for high levels, a choice coloured by their existing system which perhaps is not particularly clear and which they push harder in an attempt to compensate, but as we have seen a clear system does not necessarily have to be loud. It is important to appreciate that extra decibels might only be achieved by doubling or tripling the cost of the system.

The target sound pressure level should also indicate by how much it can vary from seat to seat, the less the variation the more expensive the system will be because more loudspeakers might be needed to achieve the smoother coverage. Nevertheless the variation should always be within 6dB because assuming that the operator is satisfied with the level where he is (and assuming he is in the auditorium) he can be secure in the knowledge that no-one in the audience is being unduly blasted or being served insufficient level. Finally target sound pressure level figure must also be expressed relative to the desired frequency response of the system; it is expensive to build loudspeakers to achieve very low frequencies.

A typical specification clause used by the author is as follows:

'The performance of the system which will be measured by the client's consultants should cover the range 50Hz to 15kHz and shall be capable of producing an rms sound pressure level over this range of —dB with an acoustic distortion level sufficiently low to ensure minimum listening fatigue; while still being able to withstand transient peaks of up to —dB. A deviation from the rms figure seat-to-seat of plus or minus 3dB will be permitted.'

The supplier should state that his equipment can match the specification, or if it cannot he should state what it can achieve in the same terms. A statement of power rating ('our loudspeaker is rated at 120 watts rms') does not tell us if it can match the required performance.

Demonstrations of individual items of equipment can be useful but sometimes the tenders are so close that it is wise to build in a clause asking for a complete system demonstration installed in the venue for a performance. Small manufacturers will find this difficult as will others if their products are custom-made and still others will find the request insulting. The good ones will comply willingly because not only will it put them in a good light but also it will provide them with an ideal opportunity of experimenting and however accurate calculations are there is no substitute for playing with the venue itself. A similar way to achieve this result is to hire a system for a production (ideally on long term reducing hire) and then negotiate a sale price once installed; but it is wiser to make any substitutions during the hire and not during the sale period.

The specification also needs to state clearly the number of microphone, effects and foldback loudspeaker points and their required locations and it is especially important in these areas to allow for future growth. A full set of drawings of each level of the building (together with vertical sections) should be made available and the specification should draw the prospective tenderer's attention to avoiding any particular

loudspeaker or mixer positions which would impede the normal working of the venue, typical cases are lighting bridges which might be impeded by loudspeaker clusters. Structural work, such as suspensions for clusters should be made the responsibility of the tenderer although the client is also legally obliged to check the calculations and fixtures.

The tenderer should also be asked to provide a schematic of the sound system and it is a good idea to mount this adjacent to control and equipment rack locations. A typical schematic for a system the author designed is shown on the next page.

Schematics like this are excellent ways of calculating the basic architecture of the system.

Sometimes the budget does not permit a whole system to be installed at one time and the purchase is phased over two or more financial years. Obviously the drawback to this method is that each new item will be prevented from delivering its best by the equipment remaining from the old system. If this approach is inevitable then all parties to the decision should be aware of the drawbacks and are prevented from vetoing next year's money because this year's equipment did not live up to expectations. Extra finance can sometimes be raised through long term leasing through finance houses, and many suppliers can help with information on this, and of course grants can often be sought from Local Authorities or National institutions. Discounts are sometimes available for payment with order and occasionally in return for free advertisements in programmes. Small items such as microphones can often be purchased in parts, budgeted as 'spares' or 'repairs and maintenance' and then assembled to make a complete unit!

Finally most new systems involve new or additional electrical work and since the majority of suppliers do not have in-house electrical contractors this area frequently forms the subject of a separate or a sub contract. One problem is that the system suppliers' requirements might all differ and so it is wiser if they can quote for this work on a subcontract basis, keeping control and alleviating the client of additional supervisory work. In these cases it is vital that the main contract binds the main contractor to be responsible for the whole system, wiring and all, not just his equipment. Where the installation is a separate contract it is important to assess the contractor's track record of sound installations since many (otherwise excellent) contractors do not understand the importance of signal separation and think consultants et al are being fussy.

The electrical installation should be given equal status with the rest of the system, especially in terms of its budget, otherwise it will be skimped and become the weak link.

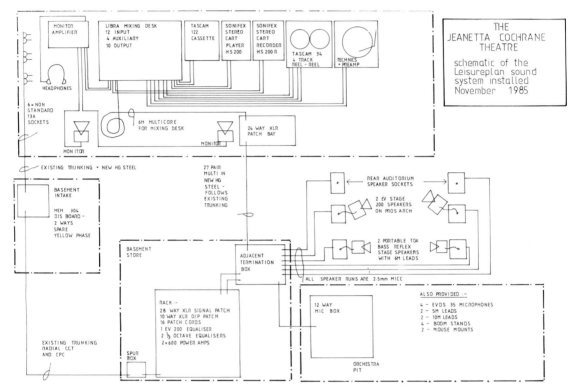

System diagram – it is very useful to prepare these to ensure all items have been considered, and also to leave a copy in the system handbook.

SECTION FIVE – COMMUNICATION AND EFFECTS SYSTEMS

COMMUNICATIONS

If sound system budgets are the poor relation in theatre financing, then communication budgets are a long-forgotten relation. Cutting back on such matters is false economy. Theatre management is partially about balancing budgets, and bad communication can waste time and tempers during the fit-up and rehearsal periods when labour is intensive, tired and expensive.

Just as there are two phases in a production, rehearsal and performance, so are there two different types of contact required between those initiating instructions (directors, designers and stage managers) and those carrying out those instructions. In rehearsal it helps if everyone can talk to everyone else, in performance there must be one person issuing cues.

CUE LIGHTS

A very simple method of indication is light, and the theatre has used this extensively in the past before the growth of sound. Before we look at the system we need to appreciate how the SM issues his instructions.

Firstly the production is divided into cues – points where the staff have to carry out some task. Next the SM will mark on his prompt copy not only the cue itself known as the 'GO', but also a warning several pages or moments in advance known as the 'STAND BY'. During operation the stand by is signalled by a red light and the go by a green light. Both lights on the SM desk and on the other end – the outstation – are wired in series so that if one fails, so does the other end and the SM knows his instruction has not got through.

The switches on the SM desk should have a positive action in keeping with their function and there are ABTT recommendations for colouring and layout.

In recent times various methods of acknowledgement have been applied to the standby circuit since the SM frequently needs to know if the outstation is manned and his cue understood.

Typical stage manager's desk layout, the cuelight buttons are colour coded.

Usually the outstation presses a small button which interrupts the circuit and causes the red light to go out momentarily. On other systems the light automatically flashes until the push is depressed at which point the light remains on.

Cue lights are still useful in areas where verbal communication is difficult, i.e. on stage. Here a portable outstation on a long lead may be preferable to a wall box, so that it can be better placed with respect to the set.

The Royal Opera House recently successfully designed and installed its own version of the cue-light system using matrices of LEDs. In their system each outstation can be 'patched' to work with others without signal loss, and the control will check that all outstations are working before the performance commences.

RING INTERCOMS

In a rehearsal the stage manager needs to talk to all his crew, and they to him, to query instructions and raise problems. The lighting designer needs to talk to the lighting operator, projection engineer and follow-spot operators and they need to be able to go back to him. The lighting operator also needs to talk to the dimmer room, and vice-versa, for maintenance – changing fuses, repairing dimmers, etc. The director too will require some communication – certainly with the stage manager, but on complex productions he may prefer to talk straight to the crew and bypass the stage manager to explain what he needs done. Finally there may be a need for sound operators and designers to talk both to equipment positioned backstage and to different parts of the auditorium to monitor quality and level.

So we have several simultaneous chains of communication with a requirement for the SM (stage manager) to override all the chains to initiate action. This need is served by the ring-intercom system, wherein each person is given a single-muff headset which is in turn fitted with a small boom mic. The unit is fed from a small amplifier belt-mounted (or built into a wall unit) and containing volume controls and a light to indicate that the wearer is needed. The system operates on the 'hands free' basis in that it can be selected to be permanently live (because most

crew will require their hands free to operate some equipment) and the more recent units use noise-cancelling mics which do not pick up the ambient noise but are sensitive only to the wearer's voice. (A regrettable trend is the production of headsets without adjustment as to which ear is covered by the muff, lighting designers at the production desk will testify that directors always seem to sit on their 'dead' side!)

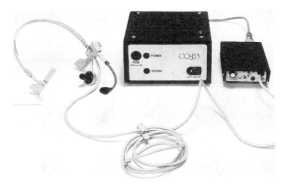

Typical lightweight headset and boom microphone with belt-pack for a ring intercom system.

Some systems provide 'crashcall' buttons, so that only one mic per chain, say, SM, lighting designer or director, may talk to that chain and cut out other mics from interrupting. Systems also provide for headsets to receive a selection of chains or a blend. This would be useful to lighting control and follow spots where instructions would emanate normally from the SM during rehearsal and show, but alterations may also come from the lighting designer who would not wish to talk to non-lighting personnel.

Ring intercoms are also useful whilst the electrical staff are rigging and focusing lamps. The simple cabling required (mic lines looped from place to place) means that new sockets may be inserted anywhere in the line, and lighting galleries, slots and boxes are easily wired for access. The crew member doing the focusing takes the headset around with him and just plugs into the nearest socket. Voices are saved and hopefully tempers kept and time respected. Another useful socket location is the orchestra pit rail where stage management sit when 'deading' the scenery, headsets here can connect to flies so that voices need not be raised and flies can reply if there are problems.

During performance the number of chains is reduced since only the SM is issuing instructions. Essentially here the talk is outward from the SM and crew need only to talk to acknowledge or notify him of an emergency.

RADIO SYSTEMS

Occasionally it is necessary to have communication with a crew member who cannot be connected by a cable. Often the crew member is operating scenery on stage, as in the famous trucks in 'Blitz' which each contained a stage manager who drove them. In this case, instructions were passed from another stage manager via radio microphone transmitter to receivers in the trucks and on to the operators via an earpiece. This was an unusual use of this equipment in its day but more people are familiar with radio microphones now and the units are easily linked for such a special occasion. It is possible to complete the chain by fitting the operator with a boom mic and transmitter so that he may talk out to the main stage manager.

Radio microphones are authorised by the DTI and it is now practical to use a large amount of different channels at the same time and it is also possible for communication purposes to tune several receivers to the same transmitter – so several crew members could all hear the same set of instructions.

The relaxation in the licensing of transmitters has brought a growth in professional walkie-talkies and CB radio. Essentially there is no reason why either should not work in a theatre, excepting that the metalwork in the fly tower usually screens out any signals, and of course CBs are prone to unwanted conversations. Hence only professional walkie-talkies should be considered and it is a good idea to hire first and check out local reception.

PAGING

Paging systems, identified in the past by a well-known brand of speaker on the wall, are far more complex than a simple speaker suggests; perhaps this is why budgets are so low. The cost in complex paging systems is not in the speakers but at the other end of the system, in the control.

Of course there are few production areas that may be paged during a performance, for example perhaps only closed electrics areas like the projection room, lighting control and sound room (although the latter really should be open to the theatre acoustic). In these circumstances the SM can issue his instructions through the paging speaker; the disadvantage of course being that the other end can't answer back unless other equipment is used.

Paging would also go to dressing rooms either as a whole circuit, or to individual rooms if stars are involved.

Paging loudspeakers receive a relay of the show from a microphone or microphones suspended downstage, often the same ones serving the hard-of-hearing system. If this is the case then the mics need to be of a much higher quality than would be the case if they were serving the backstage areas alone. Hard-of-hearing sound is picked up on the audience member's 'T' channel and transmitted either via a single loop of cable laid round the theatre, or via an infra-red system, which many users consider the more reliable although it cannot serve as many seats.

The SM's operation of his paging push brings in a relay which allows his mic to talk into the system and cuts out the show relay. The system reverses when he has finished. The best systems are those in which the dressing room speaker has a volume control which is fitted only to the show relay chain – not to the SM chain, hence the cast cannot turn off their instructions from the SM. The disadvantage of this 'SM only' volume control system is that it requires three wires (and some manufacturers need four). Simpler two-wire systems are available but with an overall volume control so that turning down the show also turns down the SM. Some units have a preset control that may also be adjusted with a screwdriver.

The SM should also be able to page backstage technical areas like crewroom, workshop and scene dock and on large or noisy stages it is an advantage if he can also page the stage itself. In these areas where high sound levels and rough conditions prevail, the horn loudspeaker is best for its rugged appearance and high efficiency. It is also useful (and sometimes a requirement of the Fire Officer) if the SM can talk to the audience during emergencies. This can be achieved through a simple system which could also have battery backup for use in power cuts. Otherwise of course the main house system could be used if the SM can have access to a mic channel.

Finally the SM needs to page the foyer and bars and here great care needs to be taken as more speakers are usually required than is often thought. These areas suffer from very high audience ambient sound levels and a good balance is required from well-distributed units; not an ineffectual muttering from one discreet box. The author has designed several systems which provide local volume controls in bars, box-offices and front-of-house management areas, each control offering a few dB adjustment dependent on audience flow. The adjustment is based on measurements of a selection of background levels (for empty, medium and full capacities) and provides 10–25dB headroom in each case.

In all cases where announcements are repeated, it is worth considering using a cassette recording made under good conditions (rather than a hasty muffled announcement made under stress). Female voices are better for this than male as they are clearer and more penetrating.

There is often a requirement for paging to be carried out from another location – say from the stage door or front-of-house office. This is easily achieved and at little extra cost, but the system must be designed so that the SM always has priority, other paging locations are usually provided with 'engaged' lights when one location is using the system. If the extra paging locations are adjacent to loudspeakers then a cut-out might also be needed to overcome local feedback.

TELEPHONES

In all the above systems the SM features as the fulcrum of the communication chain. Often, however, one part of the theatre needs to be in touch with another and the telephone is an ideal method. Generally there may be considered three systems: public, internal and stage areas. It is desirable to keep the stage areas separate from the others and likely locations are:

Stage Manager
Front of House Manager
Stage Door
Lighting Control

Sound Control
Dimmer room
Electrical workshop
Projection room
Flies
Production Desk
Stage Opposite Side
Orchestra Pit
Prop Room
Crew Room

These, of course, are merely suggestions but if the numbers are restricted from the above then these can be easily accommodated within many of the handset-only units now available and exchanges will not be needed. Telephones coupled with the ring-intercoms provide an ideal balance since together they are both versatile and discreet.

Some telephone systems connect to SM desk pushes and are linked to other facilities so that selection of a 'Performance' push cuts out all work lights, selects exits and indicator lights and switches all bells to light call. Obviously all phones within earshot of the stage and auditorium must be able to be switched to light call rather than bell.

The rest of the theatre can be accommodated as a separate internal system or within a PABX public network. It is a good idea to have coinbox telephones only in unsupervised parts of the stage and dressing room area, except for one or two public lines available to recognised priorities like designers and stage managers.

So we have discussed paging, cue lights, ring intercoms and telephones. It is important to understand that for all but the smallest theatre, these are not alternatives but merely different ways of achieving the same end, relevant to the need. Ideally a theatre should be provided with all these systems, not only so that the most appropriate system may be selected for a specific purpose but also in order to provide backup communication in the case of failure.

GENERAL FACILITIES PANELS

It is likely therefore that several locations will have many facilities available to them. One consideration in planning the system has to be access and appearance and in recent years the

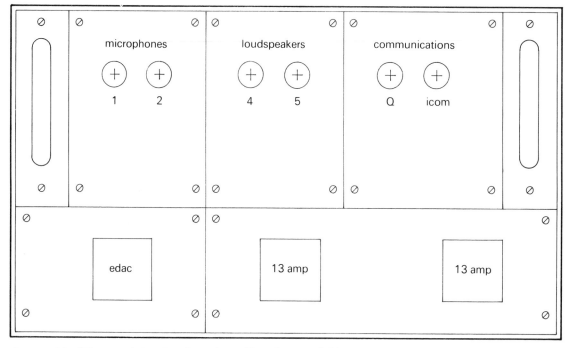

A general facilities panel showing the variety of functions available.

untidy multitude of small boxes, each carrying a different service, has been replaced by a single box carrying all the facilities and served by a multi compartment trunking. Consider the lighting control room for example. This will require a show relay speaker with volume control operable only on the relay chain but which also receives the SM, a socket and volume control for the main ring intercom of the SM and another volume control to mix in the lighting designer, a red cue light with acknowledge push and a green cue light, and finally a telephone.

Most stage general facilities panels go further than that and also carry the main sound microphone and loudspeaker sockets as well. Mains sockets are also often provided, especially for sound equipment, in which case they need residual circuit breakers.

Under these circumstances it is vital that each system uses a different connector so that no short circuits can be set up, sadly there are no generally agreed standards.

RECORDED REPRODUCTION

This book is primarily about the design of systems in which the source of sound is live, such as in the reinforcement of speech or in the form of vocal and instrument amplification on musicals and concerts. Now we will turn our attention to systems reproducing recorded sound whether the content of the recording is speech, music or sound effects.

PLAYBACK DEVICES

First it must be appreciated that the digital revolution has transformed many of the devices used, and the speed of progress limits this book to identifying current techniques and trends. Let us therefore examine the devices on which recorded sound can be played back today:

a) vinyl record (disc)
b) compact disc (CD)
c) C-cassette
d) cartridge (cart machine)
e) reel-to-reel (tape deck)
f) samplers and other digital devices

Now let us examine the advantages and disadvantages of each format:

Vinyl disc In order for analogue discs to be used during performance the player needs a precision groove locating device on the arm, the cartridge needs to be selected for 'backcueing' in coordination with a prefade listen facility. The above devices are more likely to be found on disco equipment than in a theatre (although they are now being replaced by CDs); the disc is therefore mostly used as a source from which other recordings can be made rather than for playback during the performance.

If recordings are to be made the player must be transcription standard and fitted with a method of checking that the speeds (usually 33 rpm and 45 rpm) are accurate, generally this is done with a small stroboscopic band fitted to the rim of the turntable; access to 78 rpm machines is also useful for older recordings and since these often possess surface noise some noise reduction facility in the recording process is useful in order to maximise the signal to noise ratio.

Transcription turntable from Revox.

Digitally recorded discs will already possess a good signal-to-noise ratio but of course the quality will deteriorate with consistent playing as the vinyl surface wears and attracts dust.

Compact disc Readers will now be familiar with the exceptional quality offered through these digital devices, some first think the CD sound is too 'cold' by comparison with the 'warmer' (though less accurate) sound achieved from vinyl discs – certainly good quality music is best played by CD.

There are CD machines now offering recording facilities too and although some are arranged to 'write once read many' (WORM) others will offer sophisticated editing, perhaps in time replacing the reel-to-reel machines. At the moment the machines are available in CD-R which means that the recording can only be made once, and CD-E which means that the recording can be erased.

CD effects disc, one of ten to date from Digiffects.

The durability of the quality, and the ability of the CD player to locate tracks with great accuracy has led to the commercial production of CD effects discs and if the particular effect on offer is precisely what is required then it can easily be played in the performance direct from the CD, otherwise the CD would be used to make up the main recording. (There is recent evidence that CD-R discs do deteriorate after considerable use.)

Cassette The analogue C-cassette cannot be edited and lacks facilities for the precise location of tracks. Its use therefore should be confined to background music (there are several machines which play both sides of the cassette and others which store cassettes for long periods of music).

Because C-cassettes are cheap and numerous they are often the base on which recordings for amateur shows are made. Theatres which stage amateur shows are wise to build an input panel containing a variety of connectors, Cannon, Din jack, miniature jack, phono etc, so that time is not wasted making up leads. The input panel should contain a gain control so that the next stage is not overloaded.

Digital cassette machines are now available and as expected these offer improved quality by comparison with their analogue counterparts. In time some machines will offer the ability to locate tracks precisely and this will open up the use of digital cassette machines considerably.

Cartridge The analogue cart machine was popularised by its use in playing 'jingles' on popular radio and it has now become a standard item in most theatres since it offers random access (via different carts) and ease of recording. Some carts offer the ability to store several cues, each lined up automatically by the player and others can offer long playing loops ideal for background sounds.

Cartridges showing the interior mechanism.

Popular cartridge player/recorder.

Reel-to-reel This method is the one with which people will be the most familiar for making up analogue recordings of effects and music. It is therefore wise to consider this more fully before we discuss sampling and other digital devices.

Professional reel-to-reel machine, access to the heads for editing is vital.

The process of tape recording makes use of the fluctuating magnetic field created by the fluctuating current at the recording head. This 'assembles' the tiny 'magnets' on the tape into a pattern which is readable by the playback head. The more tiny 'magnets' that pass the recording head in any second, the better will be the frequency response of the recording, so the faster the tape speed the better. Speech is acceptable at $3\frac{3}{4}$ ips but preferable at $7\frac{1}{2}$ ips which is the speed at which most theatre effects and music are recorded but improvements in performance are happening constantly and the Dolby system has also helped overall quality. Some professional machines are two speed, others three, the full speed range being $1\frac{7}{8}$, $3\frac{3}{4}$, $7\frac{1}{2}$ and 15 ips. Some machines can be fitted with a variable speed control which greatly facilitates the creation of effects. (It is worth noting here that cart machines also come in $3\frac{3}{4}$, $7\frac{1}{2}$ – the standard, and 15 ips, and that variable speed is also available.)

Like the rest of the sound system, the choice of a reel-to-reel tape deck is another area where the purchase obtains accurate value for money. The expensive professional models offer improvements over their cheaper counterparts. Unlike domestic models, professional recorders have

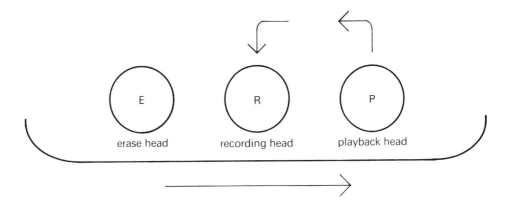

Head arrangement showing how an echo can be fed onto the tape from the playback head; this arrangement also allows a recording to be monitored as it is made.

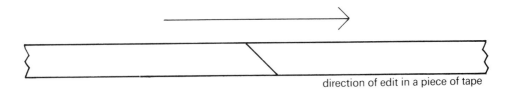

direction of edit in a piece of tape

Reel-to-reel machine in a trolley for ease of positioning adjacent to the mixer.

three heads; erase, record and play. This means that a recording can easily be monitored by the playback head as it is made; it also means that some degree of echo is possible by feeding the monitored playback to the recording head again. A professional tape recorder will also allow plenty of access to the heads so that the tape may be easily edited as it passes the playback head. A professional machine also allows for a selection of internationally agreed equalisation settings to

be applied to the tape so that standard characteristics are maintained, the NAB (National Association of Broadcasters – U.S.A.) is the most common.

EDITING ANALOGUE TAPE

The tape should be moved back and forward by hand so that the precise position on the tape of sound and silence can be judged. Cuts are made relative to the playback head and the location of the sound with special non-metallic scissors, or razor blades, and always at an angle to overcome noise on a join – this also prevents splices from coming undone. Special jointing tape and blocks must be used.

Each piece of tape containing an effect is separated from another by means of a leader tape. This should be coloured differently to the back of the recording tape (which will be the side facing the operator), different colours of leaders are helpful in locating effects on fast winding but care should be taken not to overlook the dim and coloured lighting of operating positions. The nature of the effect should be written on the leader with a chinagraph pencil. Most professional tape decks are fitted with a method of

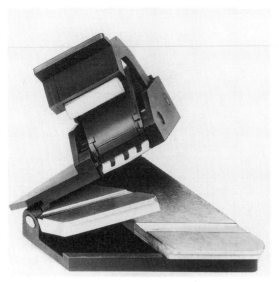

CAT automatic tape splicer, the action of the arm makes perfect 60 degree cuts and dispenses tabs of splicing tape.

automatically stopping the movement of the tape once the effect has been played. Modern units are fitted with a light sensitive cell and a small bulb, the light being allowed to pass from one to the other by the insertion in the effects tape of clear tape. Older machines were fitted with a split ring containing part of the stop circuit, which was completed when a metal foil tape was inserted into the effects tape. Although these devices are a considerable help, they are by no means totally reliable and the sound operator should be always on his guard (it is sensible to carry spares for the vital parts of the autostop circuits).

Often sound effects are continuous, birdsong being a typical example. In these cases a loop of tape is made, taking care not to produce a 'click' join or distinctive effect which would easily give the game away as it was repeated. Some designers are happy to use loops in the show – taking care that they cannot snag on the machine or adjacent items. Others prefer to set the loop to record whatever length of effect is required and cut this into the main tape. Loops are moved solely by the capstan and not by the reel motors, therefore some professional machines possess the facility to switch these off; a continuous cart would be a wiser method of achieving background sounds since unlike the loop, it cannot snag on other equipment in the control area.

The completed tape should begin with a line up tone, usually 1000Hz at 0dB, and there should be a label or announcement indicating that, so that operators can easily line up tape machines as closely as possible to that which made the original recording and a copy should always be made of the completed, edited tape.

Since control positions are frequently full of equipment, it is unlikely that the tape machines will be immediately accessible, therefore remote control over the basic functions is often provided. Again, like the auto stop, this facility is not 100 per cent reliable therefore the machine should be visible and reasonably accessible. Since machines frequently work within the audience's hearing, their operation also needs to be silent (cart machines are much quieter than reel-to-reel machines, although not totally silent).

It is wise to think in terms of two machines.

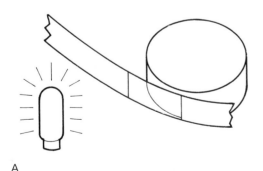

A

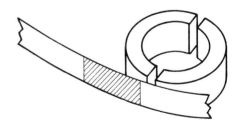

B

Automatic stops, the most common is that in A in which a light passes through a clear tape to the cell; B is older and consists of a metal foil which links two halves of a circuit ring.

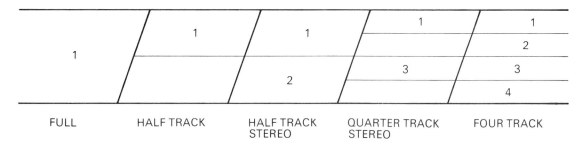

FULL   HALF TRACK   HALF TRACK STEREO   QUARTER TRACK STEREO   FOUR TRACK

TRACK CONFIGURATIONS
The five options above are those currently available on $\frac{1}{4}$" tape with half-track stereo (half-track on its own is mono) and four track being the most commonly used for theatre work. Full track is rarely used outside the recording and broadcast industries and quarter track stereo lacks the quality of the other formats.

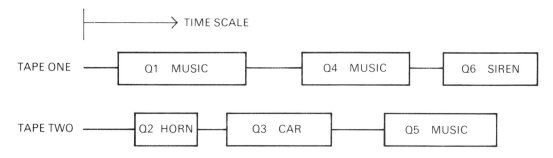

Block diagram of sound effects showing how the effects can overlap and thus on which machine the effect needs to be played.

Sometimes effects overlap, such as those of continuous background birdsong with spot effects over. On other occasions it is a good idea to play background music as the audience enter, especially in light entertainment. This really needs to be capable of playing well after the normal curtain up time, in case of a late start – hence the first effect can be lined up ready on the other machine. It is a good idea to draw a plan of the timing of effects, as above, so that the machines can be utilised to their best advantage.

These drawings will of course take account of the track configurations, and hence the number of simultaneous effects available from each machine.

Plots for effects working need to note relevant build and fade levels and rates and loudspeaker routing – it is insufficient to rely solely on the order of effects on the tape and simply push the button!

Finally all tape machines and editing blocks should be cleaned and checked regularly, dirty blocks and heads can seriously impede performance quality.

LIVE EFFECTS

Before the advent of recording, all effects were live but today few remain. Two areas that benefit from being live are the effects of bells and weather. In the first case few sound systems can accurately reproduce the attack and harmonics of a bell and the timing of telephones and doorbells in particular benefit from being operated directly by the stage manager. Hence clock chimes, doorbells, telephones and even church bells are often produced live, recordings being used only in complex or unusual cases. Timing is vital here since telephones should not ring after being answered and ideally should be wired so

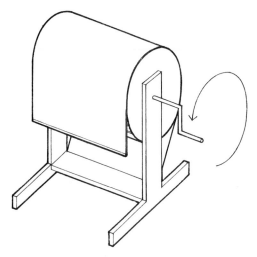

A wind machine; canvas stretched over a revolving drum; a skilled operator can produce very realistic effects.

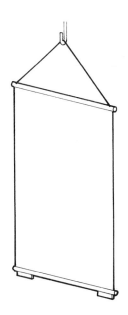

A thunder sheet suspended backstage and rattled to produce crisp cracks of thunder rather than low rumbles which were often done by cannon balls rolling down chutes.

they cannot. Small loudspeakers can be concealed in the handset for real authenticity. The effects of weather can be produced by recording but they are seldom convincing. One problem is that a recording implies a degree of repetition which is not present in reality.

Rain can be represented by the movement of dried peas in a box, wind by the turning of a slatted drum against canvas and thunder by the rattle of a piece of suspended sheet steel. Other 'noises off' include the door slam, literally a small door offstage mounted on a base board and the effect of feet treading non-wooden surfaces such as gravel, simply created by treading in a small tray fitted with stones.

Live effects are sometimes amplified but care should be taken with the frequency response of the system otherwise much of the quality will be lost. But the amplification of live effects, does not inhibit their spontaneity which can considerably add to a production. The production of live effects usually employs many people and hence they are a good way of involving volunteers and students.

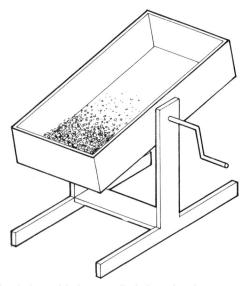

A rain box, dried peas rolled about in a box, different kinds of rain can be produced by introducing obstructions into the box.

Generally it is desirable to provide a separate loudspeaker system for recorded sound, working alongside that provided for live sound. The sources can be controlled by the same mixer that deals with the microphone channels but the live mix would be routed to separate output groups from those serving the recorded mix.

Sound effects and music have a wider frequency range than speech and therefore it is essential that the loudspeakers can accurately reproduce that range. This almost certainly will rule out line source columns and small diameter drivers for all but speech. All sound effects loud-speakers must be portable so that they can be moved closest to the location of the sound they are playing (often foldback loudspeakers can be used for economy). Although only the wealthiest theatres will be able to afford a selec-tion of effects loudspeakers it should be noted that some tailoring of the effect to its loudspeaker type is desirable. Thunder for example needs a good bass response and speech needs a smooth middle range with few crossovers in the speech frequencies. The nature of the effect will also determine the system design. For example the movement of a single source, such as a car or an aircraft implies that a mono recording, from a single track, is being crossfaded around several loudspeakers. This contrasts with a situation in which several different effects are being simul-taneously played on different loudspeakers.

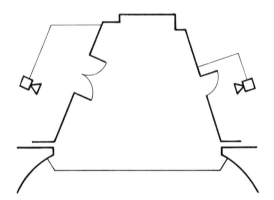

Sound effect speaker replacement; the units should face the audience as much as possible and be located near the apparent source of sound, the left speaker could be producing outdoor noises such as bird song whilst the right could produce noise of activity in an offstage room.

Sound effects should never distract the audi-ence from the play, instead they should blend with other aspects of the production. The section on operating may have already indicated some useful hints but it is worth noting that the sound levels of effects are usually set by the director and the sound operator in the middle of other techni-cal activities often when the lighting designer has control over the only headset in the stalls; a proper rehearsal time must be scheduled. Levels

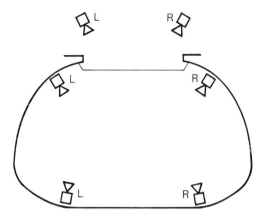

Quadrophonic effects with rear speakers and a front pair either on stage or in the auditorium. A series of different effects produced simultaneously from all four corners would be quadrophinic but one effect, i.e. an aeroplane, could be faded from one speaker to the next to create movement although the original tape would be mono.

set in an empty theatre rarely take into account the ambient noise the audience will make or the amount of sound they will soak up and so levels often have to be increased after the first public performance. If time is tight for setting levels it is wise to identify just three levels as average set-tings for quiet, medium and loud effects and simply play each effect according to one of those three basic settings, adjustments can then be made later.

DIGITAL AUDIO
(A BASIC INTRODUCTION)

The reader will (hopefully!) appreciate that the speed of the digital revolution dictates that a book has to confine itself to the basic outline because it stands no hope of keeping pace with developments, and it is assumed that the reader will be able to obtain periodical publications which inform of the latest advances.

BENEFITS

Although digital audio has been around for over fifteen years it is only in the last few years that it has moved outside the province of major studios and broadcasters. Readers will now be familiar with its application in compact discs (and in circuitry within analysers and other control equipment). Much of this growth stems from the enormous reduction in cost and therefore we should look at how digital audio affects sound system design.

The benefits of digital audio are considerable, for example by comparison with analogue audio, digital audio offers:

a) Increased signal to noise ratio and greater dynamic range. The s/n ratio of vinyl discs is about 60dB, CDs were introduced at around 85dB and DAT (digital audio tape) now offers in excess of 90dB. There is evidence however that DAT degenerates and that it is not a suitable long-term storage medium. (R-DAT is the process which uses the rotating head system similar to that used in video recorders).

b) Most types of digital recordings maintain consistent quality for longer periods.

c) Improved synchronisation between playback and control devices, through use of time codes (see MIDI).

d) Greater facility for shaping the sound and introducing effects (see SAMPLING).

e) Improved speed of editing and cue location.

f) Reduced size of components makes it possible to compact many functions within a given volume.

g) Improved scope for display and printout of audio data.

STORAGE CAPACITY

Digital audio devices convert the fluctuating analogue signals into the well-known binary format and one factor holding development back has been the enormous storage capacity that digital audio needs to maintain quality. However in recent years there has been a tremendous leap in the capacity of digital memory devices and this part of the revolution shows every sign of accelerating.

Storeage times vary from format to format (and can vary from manufacturer to manufacturer) but here are the generally accepted times ruling at the time of writing.

digital tape=	60 kbytes per minute per track full bandwidth
optical disk=	72 minutes full bandwidth stereo, or 512 minutes speech bandwidth mono
'chips', RAM cards=	2 minutes full bandwith (8 Mbyte) (as used in samplers etc)
hard disk=	1 hour speech frequency per 380 Mbyte (hard disks offer at least 800 Mbyte)
floppy disc=	1 hour full bandwidth per disc.

The Ferrograph hard-disc optical recorder-player.

DIGITAL MIXERS

We have indicated above (and in the section on recorded sound) the types of recording and playback devices, now let us look at the mixing and editing devices.

Digital mixers have existed in the recording industry for many years. Early digital mixers were in fact standard analogue devices with varying degrees of automation often using motorised faders (as many still do). The movement of the fader was recorded with the 'take' and duplicated as the tape was played back, hence the operator could concentrate on minute adjustments as he mixed the 16, or 24 and then 32 tracks down to the stereo pair. In the past even if digital mixers could have been afforded by the theatre, it could not benefit from such devices because the sound levels vary every night and early motorised faders could not easily be adjusted. It was this problem that led the author (in the early 1970s) to lead an investigation into an interface with stage lighting technology, then

The Audix assignable mixing desk, channels are assigned to the centre command module, adjusted and recorded.

by far the more advanced. We discussed the technique of 'assigning' one channel to a main control area and the utilisation of the digital fader wheel (commonly found on lighting consoles). Certainly one manufacturer present at the time has subsequently produced a very successful large assignable mixer.

Today large digital mixers are still too expensive for live working in most theatres. However some research has shown that because digital mixers can be smaller than their analogue counterparts the traditional rear-stalls mixing position can be smaller enabling an increase in seating capacity with consequent financial benefits.

The Lexicon OPUS digital editing desk.

Some manufacturers offer very affordable programs which convert PCs (typically Atari and Macintosh) into small digital mixers, the operation of which is via the PC's mouse. Such mixers are usually confined either to the production of sound effects or the control over playback and effects devices.

Like digital mixers on which they are based, digital editing devices have, until recently, remained within the province of the major studios. However prices are coming down. Currently the editors comprise a small digital mixer (usually 8 track), a degree of internal memory on hard or floppy disc, and the screen (typically VDU or LCD) and its associated computer QWERTY controls.

The Yamaha DMP7 incorporates effects and automation.

There are at the moment essentially two ways to edit. Devices which utilise extensive memory tend to leave the recordings unedited but memorise instructions as to which part of each recording to use in the finished product, these are called soft-edits. Other devices play the sound and offer the facility to remove unwanted sounds at the touch of a button (called hard-edits) a 'jog' wheel enables the sound to be slowly moved back and forth for precise editing in the same way that one would do when editing an analogue tape on a reel-to-reel machine. Most editors offer the ability to work on eight tracks simultaneously; care is needed because some devices permit access to many tracks but can only play any eight simultaneously – thus a '32 channel editor' might only be an 8 channel mixer.

SAMPLING

The term sampling actually refers to the computer's practice of taking regular samples of the audio signal and converting those samples into a digital signal. If the audio signal is fairly constant then it would not matter if the samples were comparatively widely spaced. However if the audio signal varies considerably then it would be wiser to sample at a greater frequency and the rate at which devices sample can vary, the higher the sampling rate the more storage is needed. Typical sampling rates at the moment are 44.1kHz for CD, 40kHz for RAM cards, 30kHz and 44.1kHz for hard disc.

MIDI

Samplers usually work with other devices, such as synthesizers and in order that each device is in sychronisation with the other, there are various agreed international time codes on to which the devices can be locked. For example SMPTE was developed for the video industry and which relates to the number of frames per second. It can be interfaced with MIDI which stands for Music Instrument Digital Interface and which is the most common timecode for audio work.

The MIDI timecode can be provided either by any device within the system so equipped or by an external synchroniser to which other MIDI based devices can be connected. The MIDI

system offers considerable scope for the musician now using digital drum kits, effects boxes and synthesizers and recording the whole on digital audio tape and a good synchroniser allows a multiplicity of prerecorded effects (such as chord, arpeggio, and double-tracking) to be brought in precisely on time, as well as the ability to select the various accepted sampling frequencies of the different devices. MIDI is also useful when 'click-tracks' are used, these are generally employed in musicals and pantomimes where the chorus' singing (and occasionally the leads!) are on tape and the start of the tape machine needs to be timed to coincide with the live musicians in the pit. The 'click', usually a metronome beat, is recorded on one track and the vocals on another, but now a track with MIDI can better synchronise the electronic sections of the orchestra.

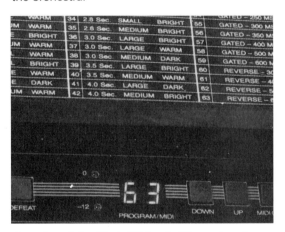

A section of the Alesis Midiverb, 63 reverberation settings at a touch.

As musicians and engineers become experienced in the use of MIDI there is evidence that many regard it as too slow (it samples at 31.25 thousand bits per second) and criticise its quality and quantity. In time therefore it may be that some kind of super MIDI will be produced.

Sampling devices have also become more affordable and offer considerable scope for the production of sound effects. These devices permit small amounts of a single sound to be stored, typically up to two minutes at the time of writing (although larger amounts can be stored via disks). The stored sound can then be adjusted in a variety of ways, for example it can

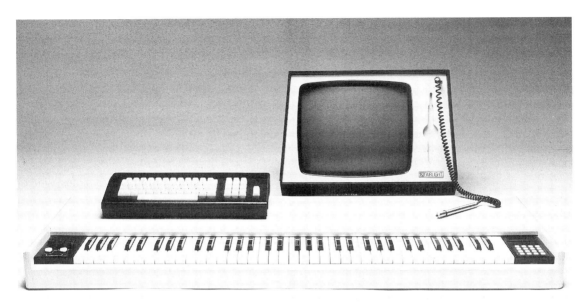

The Fairlight Musical Computer Instrument, (MCI) sampling at its best.

be played at different speeds, played at a different pitch and delay, echo and reverberation are also available. The sampler can set up loops between any two points in the sound effect. Many devices offer the facility to re-record the initial or adjusted sound on another track as though the sound was in a duet with itself.

Samplers offer considerable scope and some unscrupulous users have recorded popular music and then altered the sound to form the basis for their own track. At all times the copyright of the individual must be respected and samplers must be used only for sounds which are either in the user's own copyright or in the public domain.

PERFORMING RIGHTS

It is appropriate at this point to consider copyright. In the U.K. the law requires that a licence is needed to play any type of recorded music in public (and this includes 'members only' clubs). Royalties may also be payable, all queries can be directed to and licences obtained from:

PPL (Phonographic Performance Ltd)
Ganton House, 14–22 Ganton Street
London W1V 1LB

(*representing the recording industry*)

and also

PRS (Performing Rights Society)
29–33 Berners Street, London W1P 4AA

(*representing composers and music publishers*)

It is worth noting that the U.K. Copyright Act of 1956 is currently under review.

THINGS TO COME...

The years during which this book will be available promise to be the most exciting in terms of developments.

In 'Sound for Theatres' in 1981 I listed a number of technological advances of which many consultants were dreaming and for which I was severely criticised for being too idealistic; today most of those dreams have come true! So here goes ... already digital editing desks are using touch sensitive screens, how long before motorised fader desks are replaced with this technology? Fibre optics are already well-known in video and communication systems but as yet unknown in theatre audio, yet their installation would eradicate most of the problems associated with cabling as it exists now, and fibre optics would offer the ability to deliver much more down the same line. Supermagnets and axial weave materials could transform the loud-speaker, I have a loudspeaker in my office which is as thin as the paper on which this is being printed, superchips and organic memories promise to transform the digital revolution again.

Undoubtedly it will be digital audio which will bring about the biggest changes and at the moment the science threatens to be hijacked by computer scientists away from acousticians and sound operators. Perhaps the next few years will also see a new breed of sound system designer. Certainly sound has been very much the poor relation in terms of training and after all the best system can be poorly operated. At last there are signs that here too the next few years will see improvements.

AFTERWORD

A sound system is the most important vehicle for the production's communication with its audience and therefore the design process must be respected. Every link in the audio chain is vital in achieving a high standard of intelligibility and fidelity, any compromise and a weak link will let the others down, any ignorance or haste and the marriage between acoustics and equipment might fail. Hopefully this book has equipped the reader to enter the sound debate with clear objectives in mind.

SECTION SIX – APPENDICES

Glossary

The following is provided as quick reference to the meaning of some of the basic terms used in the various sections and in each case there is an indication of where in the book, further reading can be found by indicating the page number where the first use of the particular term occurs. The term may be used again later and for other references please see the main index.

Absorption, Insulation
see pages 28 and 30

Absorption relates to the treatment of surfaces so that they may reflect more or less sound. Insulation relates to the way in which a surface may be treated to prevent sound from passing into another room. (The calculation of the amount of absorption is one of the fundamentals of reverberation).

Ambient level
see page 16

The sound pressure level generated in an area from air-conditioning, audience etc, (i.e. the background level) excluding the level of the sound system.

Ambiophony, Assisted Resonance
see page 23

Two systems of prolonging the reverberation time by electronic means.

Amplitude
see page 12

The strength of a vibration, more amplitude means more sound.

Articulation loss
see page 92

Process of calculating system parameters so that the vital consonants are not lost.

Attenuator pad
see page 63

Device which reduces the signal flowing through a circuit, commonly found built-in to connectors in values of 10dB from 10dB to 60dB

Auxiliaries, Echo Send Foldback
see page 51

A section of the input channel which routes part of the signal to other areas or devices, notably to add echo or to enable musicians to monitor their performance by means of a separate sound system (foldback).

Balanced unbalanced
see page 74

An unbalanced line is one where there are only two signal carrying conductors, one of which is the shield. In the balanced line the shield, which is earthed, is in addition to two conductors. Balanced lines are less prone than unbalanced to interference.

Bandpass
see page 58

A filter where the response curves towards and then away from the selected frequency.

Bi-amping
see page 70

Process whereby the amplifiers are placed in the system after the crossover, and thus one each per LF and HF unit and producing a cleaner sound than if a single amp had been placed before the crossover.

Boundary mic

see pressure zone mic

Cannon
see page 75

metal connector usually associated with microphones, but also used for loudspeakers, intercoms, cuelights etc. Interchangeable with several other manufacturers' products.

Cannon

commercial name for a sub-base system

Cardioid Hypercardioid
see page 43

A microphone which is most sensitive in front, generally the one used for stage work. Hypercardioids are also known as 'rifle' mics. The term supercardioid is also used.

Cartridge

'cart', see page 118

Cassette

C-Cassette, see page 117

Clipping
see page 60

(amplitude distortion) occurs when a unit (usually the amplifier) cannot handle the excessive amount of signal fed to it.

Cluster
see page 89

Generic name for a single collection of loudspeakers centrally hung in an auditorium.

Colouration

term used to indicate audible alterations to the sound arising from the response pattern of a mic or loudspeaker.

Compact disc

CD, see page 117.

Compressor

see limiter.

Condenser
see page 41

A mic where the signal induces the interaction of a moving diaphragm and a fixed plate, the two forming a capacitor. These mics are very sensitive and produce the most even response of any kind of mic.

Constant directivity
see page 70

A loudspeaker (typically but not exclusively), a horn in which the beam does not become more directional as the frequency rises.

Critical distance
see page 94

The distance from the loudspeakers at which the level of the sound system and the level of the reverberant sound are equal. No member of the audience should be further away from the loudspeakers than this.

Crossover
see page 70

Device which separates parts of the audio signal, typically the LF and HF; crossovers set at fixed frequencies are 'passive', those which can be adjusted are 'active'.

Cue light
see page 112

Method of cueing by the stage manager which employs red lights for 'standby' and green for 'go', both the SM's lights and those on the outstation are in series to detect failures.

dB LAeq

EEC measurement of exposure to sound levels in 8 hours

Decibel (dBA)
see page 14

A measure of the difference between two other measurements, one of which may be an agreed international reference point and therefore not stated. Used to compare two sound pressure levels, 2 currents or 2 voltages.

Dolby
see page 64

Commercial name for process whereby background noise is reduced during the recording and playback process.

Digital Delay Line
see page 65

An electronic device which delays the signal to part of the sound system so that it may emerge in sympathy with the live sound (see Haas).

Diversity
see page 46

A radio mic system that employs two aerial positions per mic, the system hunts for the most suitable and 'locks on' to that offering the strongest reception.

**Direct injection
DI**
see page 87

Process whereby a signal is taken from a keyboard or guitar etc, direct (via a connector box) to the mixer.

Dynamic mic
see page 41

Otherwise known as moving coil, signal is induced by action of a moving diaphragm and coil within the poles of a magnet.

Earth loop
see page 78

Literally a loop of earthing created by a continuous circuit of mains and cables shields which becomes sensitive to radio and mains interference.

Echo send

see auxiliaries

**Echo unit/
Reverberation**
see page 22

A device which causes the whole word to be repeated. Compare with...
a process whereby the last syllable in each word is extended or deepened.

Electret mic
see page 42

variation on the condenser where the capacitor is given a permanent charge when manufactured, these mics therefore need no power supply.

Eq cut

a push on a mixer which cuts out the mixer's equalisation enabling the actual sound to be compared with the corrected sound. See above.

Equalisation
see page 51

The area of control over tonal response, mixers may have simple controls over bass and treble or sophisticated control over specific frequencies.

Equaliser
see page 58

A device which contains filters by which the frequency response of the sound can be changed.

Feedback, Howlround
see page 63

The high pitched squeal, or ringing caused by sound finding its way out of the loudspeaker back to the mic and out of the speakers again. It can be lessened by lowering the volume and/or evening out the peaks in the frequency response of the system. Directional mics and speakers are fundamental in helping to overcome this. Frequency shifters can also help.

Flat

term used to describe an even response, one in which no frequency is accentuated.

Flutter echoes
see page 25

Flutter echoes are caused by parallel walls and prevent sounds from dying away as quickly as might be desirable. (Parallel walls can be useful to music.)

Foldback
see page 51

process whereby part or all of the mix is fed back to the artists on stage via monitors and wedge loudspeakers so that they can judge their performance (see auxiliaries).

Frequency
see page 11

The number of times a source vibrates in one second. Measured in Hertz, Hz, quantities of 1000 as kHz. High frequencies vibrate many times each second, low frequencies vibrate much less.

Frequency Shifter, Phase Inverter
see page 63

Two devices which are sometimes used to reduce the system's liability to feedback. Frequency shifters adjust the output by 5Hz and Phase Inverters invert the polarity of the loudspeaker signal in pulses.

Fundamental, Harmonics
see page 13

The initial vibration is the fundamental, harmonics are the subsequent vibrations which are at equal multiples. Thus a fundamental of 100Hz will have harmonics at 200Hz, 300Hz and so on.

Gain, Sensitivity
see page 49

The control which regulates the amount of sound the channel is receiving.

Graphic
see page 58

A filter usually comprised of band-pass filters whose control knobs represent the shape of the resultant sound curve.

Grazing Effect
see page 27

The way in which sound is absorbed by the audience, stepping or raking the seating reduces the absorption, and improves sight lines.

Group, Subgroups
see page 52

The section of a mixer where the sound is brought together in combinations, (subgroups) which can then be further combined into the main output (groups).

Haas effect
see page 65

Relationship of delayed amplified sound to live sound so that the brain 'shifts' the amplified sound to line up with the live sound which arrives at the listener first. (See digital delay line.)

Harmonics

see fundamentals

Headroom
see page 61

The capacity of a device above its normal operating level in which it can permit peaks to pass undistorted.

HF, Tweeter
see page 69

The high frequency loudspeaker unit or driver

Horn, HF horn
see page 70

A loudspeaker in which the coil is attached to a metal diaphragm which excites the air in front of it, this is attached to the metal horn itself. Horns are more efficient than moving coil units and deal with the middle and upper frequencies.

House curve
see page 60

The response of the acoustic of an auditorium to pink noise, this will indicate at which frequency the system will feedback (that most prominent) and can also identify other defects in the acoustics or system.

Howlround

see feedback

Hypercardioid

see cardioid

Input Channel
see page 47

That section of a mixer which receives the signal from microphone, tape deck etc.

Insulation

see absorption

Inverse square law
see page 17

The law governing the fall off in sound pressure level as the distance from the sound or loudspeaker increases, for point sources the SPL drops 6dB for every doubling of the distance.

LF, Woofer, Bass Bin
see page 69

The low frequency unit or driver. Extended frequency systems are also known as sub-basses.

Limiter, Compressor
see page 64

Two separate devices, often combined which can control the highest and lowest levels of sound volume to defined limits.

Line source column
see page 68

A loudspeaker where the drivers are vertically mounted, often the outer ones receive less signal. These units produce even, flat topped wide beams with little fall off of SPL over distance.

Low Impedance, 100v line
see page 62

The way in which the amplifier produces its signal. Constant Voltage (100v in the U.K.) usually associated with public address because of its inferior quality. The alternative is Low Impedance which refers to the resistance offered to the circuit by the loudspeaker and in which the impedance of the speakers must match the amplifier.

Mic/Line
see page 48

Input levels for different sources offering two alternative uses for one channel, line level is an agreed international level for tape decks etc.

MIDI
see page 126

Musical Instrument Digital Interface, the commonly used timecode onto which digital audio devices may be locked.

Modular mixer
see page 57

A mixer which is assembled from a number of plug-in sections. These mixers are usually more versatile and easier to maintain than those constructed from a singe fascia.

Monitor
see page 71

A monitor speaker is a wide range unit of exceptional quality, typically with HF horn and LF moving coil unit; it can also be taken to refer to a small relay speaker in control rooms.

Moving coil loudspeaker
see page 67

The loudspeaker which produces sound vibrations by the interaction of a coil acting within a magnet, the coil being connected to the speaker cone.

NAB
see page 119

National Association of Broadcasters, U.S.A. organisation which issues standards for equipment.

Noise reduction
see page 64

System whereby the background sound is reduced, typically used in tape recording (see Dolby).

Noise gate
see page 64

A device which allows sound to pass only when a predetermined level has been reached.

Normalled
see page 77

Process whereby jacks in a patchpanel are wired so that the signal follows a 'normal' route unless interrupted by the insertion of the jack.

Notch
see page 58

A filter that operates a correction at a very specific frequency leaving those around it largely unaffected.

Octave
see page 13

Two frequencies, one of which is double the other, are separated by one octave; the two would be said to be in tune.

Output, mic sensitivity
see page 45

The amount of signal that a mic can generate. Expressed two ways, either in decibels in which case the lower the number the more sensitive the mic. Or in millivolts in which case the higher the value the more sensitive the mic.

Overload
see page 52

An LED on a mixer input, set by the manufacturer and which indicates when the channel's overload point has been reached, when the channel has run out of 'headroom'.

Q
see page 93

The ratio of a loudspeaker's vertical beam angle to its horizonal beam angle (see 6dB down point).

Pad

see attenuator

Paging
see page 114

process of issuing instructions to dressing rooms etc, via loudspeakers

Pan
see page 52

Control on a mixer which allows a mono sound to be routed as stereo.

Parametric
see page 58

A filter that can alter the frequency or rate of attentuation.

Phase inverter

see frequency shifter

Pitch
see page 13

The frequency by which a note can be identified, 'Concert Pitch' indicates that an instrument has been tuned to 440Hz (although other variations apply worldwide).

Pink noise,
White noise
see page 60

equal amounts of sound per frequency
equal amounts of sound per octave

Point source
see page 68

A source of sound (usually referring to a design of loudspeaker) the pressure level of which obeys the Inverse Square Law, i.e. it falls off 6dB with each doubling of the distance.

Polar Diagram, Pickup
see page 42

The way in which a mic 'hears' its source, the area in which it is sensitive (sometimes known as on axis).

Pre/Post
see page 51

Method by which auxiliaries' effect can be independent or dependent on the main channel fader (see auxiliaries).

Pressure zone mics PZM
PCC
see page 81

Microphones which carry with them small reflective surfaces which improves response.

PFL pre fade listen
see page 51

Facility to listen to the channel without the audience doing so, useful to check radio mics and line up tapes.

PPM meter

see Vu meter

Radio Mics
see page 45

Microphones which operate from small transmitters often concealed about the actor or within the mic itself. The result is a wire-free performance. Radio mics are licensed by the DTI. Their use is not as simple as appears and great care is necessary (see diversity).

Reel-to-reel

'tape deck', see page 118

Reflection
Reflectors
see page 23

The behaviour of sound waves relative to a particular surface. Concave surfaces focus and can lead to echoes, convex surfaces disperse. Concert platforms and modern theatres are provided with reflectors to disperse the sound so that the direct sound waves are enhanced.

Response–Flat
see page 45

The way in which a microphone de-emphasizes or accentuates particular frequencies. A flat response is an even response and usually the most desirable, although some HF lift for vocals and strings is also popular.

Reverberation
see page 22

The way in which a sound bounces around an auditorium after its original source has been cut off. The amount depends on auditorium shape, strength of signal and how much absorption is present.

Reverberation Time
see page 22

The time sound takes to die away by a defined amount, namely 60dB. There are ideal times for music and speech for a given volume.

Reverberation unit

see echo

Ribbon mic
see page 43

Mic in which a strip of corrugated foil is mounted on a coil within the poles of a magnet. These mics have a figure of eight pickup pattern and are rarely used in theatre.

Ring intercom
see page 113

combined headset and mic system in which all wearers can talk and listen simultaneously.

RMS
see page 61

The output of the amplifier taken as an average (or root mean square).

Rt60

abbreviation for Reverberation time, see above

Sampling
see page 126

process of taking regular samples of the analogue audio signal and converting them into digital signals, devices which offer process to then alter the sound sampled are known as samplers.

Sense of Direction
see page 11

High frequency sounds are more directional than low frequency sounds. The ear can detect horizontal changes of direction better than vertical changes unless given some visual clue.

Sensitivity

see gain

Show relay
see page 114

literally a system whereby the show is relayed, typically to dressing rooms although this can also mean the relay to hard-of-hearing systems.

Signal to Noise ratio
see page 57

the ratio of the programme signal to that of the noise in the system, expressed in decibels as s/n

6dB down point
see page 68

The boundary at which the SPL of a loudspeaker falls 6dB from that measured on axis 1 metre from the unit.

Slope

the rate of attenuation, expressed in dBs per octave.

Sound Pressure Levels
see page 16

The measurement of what sound we hear expressed in decibels by comparison to a zero level (actually the pressure level of a 1000Hz tone). A meter which hears as the human ear does expresses the measurement as dBA, on the 'A' scale.

Sound shadow
see page 91

Area in which whole or part of the loudspeaker beam is obstructed by scenery or architecture, typical is the shadowing of the rear stalls by the circle.

Speed
see page 12

The speed relates to the air temperature which should always be quoted. At 14°C the speed is 1115' or about 340m. The speed may be calculated by: speed = wavelength × frequency. The speed rises or falls 2' for each degree centigrade change.

Standing Waves
see page 26

Standing waves are accentuations of a set of frequencies whose wavelengths are exact multiples of the room's basic dimensions. They are usually harmful for live working, if a mic is placed at the point of accentuation its tendency to feedback is increased.

Subgroups	see groups
Transient *see page* 14	The way in which a source behaves when first vibrated. The start of the first vibration is called the attack, the duration is the sustain and the final part is the decay. String instruments tend to decay notes whereas wind instruments tend to sustain them.
Unbalanced	see balanced
Vinyl disc	see page 117
Vu and PPM *see page* 55	The two ways in which the amount of current flowing through the system can be measured. Vu meters indicate a percentage of the channel use and are faster than the PPM which has a seven point scale. Most operators prefer the PPM.
Wavelength *see page* 11	The distances from a point to the same point in another vibration. High frequencies have short wavelengths, low frequencies have long wavelengths. The length of waves we can hear range from 1″ to 40′ (2.5cm to 12.25 m).
Wedge *see page* 71	A special wedge shaped speaker for stage working in the foldback system.
White noise	see pink noise

TECHNICAL DATA

This section reproduces data in the book and also adds other helpful information.

Sound Pressure Level
see page 15

Relative to zero level, 1000Hz tone, 0dB.

Electrical Power level
see page 15

Relative to 0.001 watt or 0.775 volts across 600 ohm.

Human Voice
Fundamentals
see page 16

Bass	85–340Hz
Baritone	90–380Hz
Tenor	125–460Hz
Alto	130–680Hz
Contralto	180–600Hz
Soprano	225–1000Hz
Male Speech	125Hz
Female Speech	210Hz
Trained Male Speech	140Hz
Trained Female Speech	230Hz
Fundamentals	125–250Hz
Vowels	350–2000Hz
Consonants	1500–4000Hz

Human Voice Power
see page 16

62.5–500Hz	60% of power of voice, 5% intelligibility
500–1000Hz	35% of power, 35% intelligibility
1000–8000Hz	5% of power, 60% intelligibility
Whisper	30dBA
Conversation	50dBA
Lecturer	60dBA
Actor	70dBA

(all measured at 10′ (3m))

Human Ear
see page 18

Best range when young, pure tones, 16Hz–20kHz. Most sensitive, 3kHz–5kHz range.
Minimum chance in intensity detectable under ideal conditions, 1dB, normally about 2dB.

**High Sound Level
Exposure**
see page 18

Tables of Exposure to Industrial Noise

U.K.

90dBA	8 hr per day max.
93dBA	4 hr per day max.
96dBA	2 hr per day max.
99dBA	1 hr per day max.
102dBA	$\frac{1}{2}$ hr per day max.
105dBA	$\frac{1}{4}$ hr per day max.

U.S.A. (OSHA 1970)

90dBA	8 hr per day max.
95dBA	4 hr per day max.
100dBA	2 hr per day max.
105dBA	I hr per day max.
110dBA	$\frac{1}{2}$ hr per day max.
115dBA	$\frac{1}{4}$ hr per day max.

Reverberation Times
see page 22

Measured at full capacity and in 500Hz–100Hz band.

Covent Garden	1.2 seconds
Free Trade Hall Manchester	1.6 seconds
Royal Festival Hall	1.6 seconds
Royal Albert Hall	2.9 seconds
Teatro La Scale Milan	1.2 seconds

Ideal Volumes and Areas
see page 22

Max per seat for speech from 2.3m³ to 4.3m³ (80 to 150ft³), best option per seat for speech 3.1m³ (110 cu.ft), max per seat for music from 4.5m³ to 7.4m³ (160 to 260ft³), best option for music 5.7m³ (200ft³), max for pit musician in area 1.0m² to 1.5m².

Sabine Formula for RT
see page 28

Reverberation Time =

$$\frac{0.16 \text{ (metric constant)} \times \text{volume in metres}}{\text{total absorption in sabin metric units}}$$

The imperial formula is:

Reverberation Time =

$$\frac{0.05 \times \text{volume in cubic feet}}{\text{total absorption in square feet sabin units}}$$

Sample Absorption Coefficients
see page 28

	250Hz	500Hz	1000Hz
Brick	0.04	0.02	0.04
Concrete	0.02	0.02	0.04
Plaster	0.03	0.02	0.03
Thick carpet	0.25	0.05	0.05
Air/m³	nil	nil	0.003
Audience in upholstered seat	0.04	0.46	0.46
Empty wood seat	nil	0.15	nil
Rostrum/m²	0.1	nil	nil

Reduction Indices of Walls etc
see page 30

4" (100mm) brick plastered both sides	40dB
9" (230mm) brick plastered both sides	52dB
4" brick walls, (50mm) cavity and both sides plastered	56dB
6" concrete block, solid and plastered	50dB
$\frac{3}{8}$" (10mm) gypsum wall board	26dB
$\frac{1}{2}$" (13mm) gypsum wall board	28dB
$\frac{5}{8}$" (16mm) gypsum wall board	31dB
Partition of $\frac{3}{8}$" plastered gypsum with 4" cavity	43dB

Time Delay Calculations
see page 65

Time delay is required if the direct and amplified sound paths to a point (or two amplified paths to a point), differ by a time of more than 40 ms. This represents about 40' at a temperature of 14°C. The Haas effect (see text) denotes levels relative to maintaining the direction effect of the source.

Decibels
see page 14

Adding two sound pressure levels that are the same, add 3dB, that is two leves of say 60dB will give a level of 63dB, adding two that are not the same.

Difference in Signals	Add to Larger Signal
1dB	2.5dB
2	2.1
3	1.7
4	1.4
5	1.1
6	0.97
7	0.79
8	0.63
9	0.51
10	0.43
11	0.35
12	0.26

Distance
see page 15

Each time the distance from a point sound source is doubled the sound pressure level falls by 6dB. This does not take into account the contribution from the acoustic which would prevent any loss of some distance from the source where reverberation would take over (Inverse Square Law).

Power
see page 73

Each time the power to a loudspeaker is halved the level of intensity falls by 3dB and the SPL falls by 6dB (and vice versa if the power is doubled).

watts = volts × amps

volts = amps × ohms

volts² = ohms × watts

Number of Mics Live
see page 107

Each time the number of live microphones is doubled the sound level is effectively reduced by 3dB otherwise feedback could result.

Cable Guide
see page 75

8 ohm 50m up to 100w	0.75m²
8 ohm 50m 100w to 400w	2.5m²
8 ohm 50m 400w to 1000w	4.0m²
100v line up to 100w	0.5m²
100v line 100w to 1000w	1.0m²

(refers to the ABTT data sheet)

Plug and Socket Guide
see page 75

Mic level carried are male, even numbers (XLR – 3 – 12c). Speaker level carriers are usually female, odd numbers (XLR – 4 – 11c).

Mic carriers are three pin, speakers three or four pin (see text).

Articulation Loss
see pages 93 *and* 94

$$\% \, Alcons = \frac{200(D2)^2 \times (Rt60)^2 \times (n+1)}{volume \times Q \text{ of loudspeakers} \times M}$$

where **% Alcons** = % of lost consonants
D2 = distance from the loudspeaker
to the furthest audience member
Rt60 = Reverberation time
n = number of loudspeaker groups
V = volume in cubic metres
M = usually 1 (see text)

minimum Q for
15% Alcons $= \dfrac{200 \, (D2)^2 \times (Rt60)^2 \times (n+1)}{15 \times volume \times M}$

maximum distance
to loudspeaker $= \sqrt{\dfrac{15 \times volume \times Q \times M}{200(Rt60)^2 \times (n+1)}}$

maximum Rt for
15% Alcons $= \sqrt{\dfrac{15 \times volume + Q \times M}{200 \times (D2)^2 \times (n+1)}}$

Q of loudspeakers
see page 93

$$Q = \frac{180°}{arc \, sin \left(\dfrac{sin \text{ horizontal angle}}{2} \times \dfrac{sin \text{ vertical angle}}{2} \right)}$$

Critical Distance
see page 94

$$DC = 0.03121 \sqrt{\frac{Q \times volume \times M \, (1\text{-constant})}{Rt60 \times (n+1)}}$$

Conversion Factors

to convert					
	metres	into	*feet*	multiply by	**3.28**
	feet	into	*metres*	multiply by	**0.305**
	square metres	into	*square feet*	multiply by	**10.8**
	square feet	into	*square metres*	multiply by	**0.093**
	cubic metres	into	*cubic feet*	multiply by	**35.3**
	cubic feet	into	*cubic metres*	multiply by	**0.0283**

commonly used metric prefixes			
	milli	**m**	one thousandth
	micro	μ	one millionth
	kilo	**k**	one thousand
	mega	**M**	one million

BIBLIOGRAPHY

Here is a selection of books and periodicals that are available to take the reader further into the subject of theatre sound. The list is not exhaustive but in many cases the books form standard reference works on a particular aspect.

*Note also that many manufacturers also provide handbooks on acoustics, system design and product use, notably Altec, AKG, Electrovoice, BASF.

**Also note that the Audio Engineering Society publishes many papers on acoustics and equipment: AES, Lent Rise Road, Burnham, Slough, SL1 7NY.

ACOUSTICS

Detailing for Acoustics
Lord & Templeton, Architectural Press

Guide to Acoustic Practice
BBC Engineering

Architectural Acoustics
K B Ginn, Bruel and Kjaer

Noise
Rupert Taylor, Pelican

Acoustics, Noise and Buildings
Parking and Humphreys, Faber

Applied Acoustics
G. Porges, Arnold

Design for Good Acoustics and Noise Control
J E Moore, Macmillan

Auditorium Acoustics
Robin Mackenzie, Applied Science

Music, Acoustics and Architecture
Leo Beranek, Wiley

Environmental Acoustics
Leslie L Dooelle, McGraw Hill

MICROPHONES

Microphones
A E Robertson, Iliffe

Microphones, How They Work and How to Use Them
Martin Clifford, Foulsham

The Use of Microphones
Alec Nisbett, Focal Press

LOUDSPEAKERS

Loudspeakers
G A Briggs

Loudspeaker and Headphone Handbook
John Borwick, Butterworths

Loudspeakers
E J Jordan, Focal Press

VOICE

Clear Speech
Malcom Morrison, A & C Black

Voice and Speech in the Theatre
Clifford Turner, Pitman

The Pronunciation of English
Daniel Jones, Cambridge Press

Speech Science
Richard Hoops, Thomas

Speech Training
C V Burgess, English University Press

Your Voice and How to Use it
Cicelly Berry, Harrap

ELECTRONIC MUSIC

Electronic Music Productions
Alan Douglas, Tab Books

Backstage Rock
Clem Gorman, Pan

RECORDING AND EFFECTS

Tape Recording
Wallace Sharps, Fountain

Noises off
Frank Napier, Garnet Miller

High Quality Sound Production and Reproduction
Burrell Haddon, Iliffe

Manual of Sound Recording
John Alfred, Fountain

Music in Modern Media
R E Dolan, Schirmer

SYSTEM DESIGN

Audio Systems Designer
Mapp & Goosens, Klark Teknik

Audio Systems Handbook
Norman Crowhurst, Tab Books

Public Address Handbook
Vivian Capel, Fountain Press

Stage Sound
David Collision, Studio Vista

Sound System Engineering
Don and Carolyn Davis, Sams Inc.

Sound in the Theatre
Meyer and Mallory, Audio Library

ELECTRONICS

A Dictionary of Electronics
S. Handel, Penguin

Electronics
Roland Worcester, Hamlyn

Electronics Made Simple
Henry Jacobowitz, W H Allen

PERIODICALS

Lighting and Sound International (monthly)
PLASA, 7 Highlight House, St Leonards Rd,
Eastbourne

Sightline (May and November)
ABTT, 4 Gt. Pulteney Street, London W1

Cue International (bi-month)
5 River Park Estate, Berkhampstead, Herts

The Stage (weekly)
The Stage, 47 Bermondsey Street, London SE1

Theatre Crafts (bi-monthly)
PO Box 470, Mt Morris, IL 61054-0470, U.S.A.

Sound and Communications (monthly)
Dennis Publishing, 14 Rathbone Place, London W1

Sound Engineer and Producer (monthly)
100 Avenue Road, London NW3

Studio Sound (monthly, free to professional
engineers etc.)
Link House, Dingwall Avenue, Croydon, Surrey

USEFUL ADDRESSES

This is an almost impossible list to compile because there is no certain way of including everyone, ensuring that addresses are always up-to-date or of featuring new companies. Hence we suggest that the addresses below will form a good point of contact backed up by the periodicals listed earlier.

The Association of British Theatre Technicians
(ABTT)
4 Great Pulteney Street, London W1

The United States Institute of Theatre Technology
(USITT)
8–10 West 19th Street Suite 5-A, New York,
NY 10011

Professional Lighting and Sound Association
(PLASA)
7 Highlight House, St Leonards Road, Eastbourne

Sound and Communications Industries Federation
(SCIF)
4b High Street, Burnham, Slough SL1 7JH

PHOTOGRAPH ACKNOWLEDGEMENTS

AKG Acoustics
Allen and Heath
Amcron
Audix
Bose
Brooks Photography
Court Acoustics
Cyco systems
Digiffects
Dolby
EDC
Electrosonic
EMO Systems
Fox Waterman Photography
FWO Bauch
Ian B Albery
Klark Teknik
Leisureplan
Libra Electronics
Lynton Black photography

Mason Bryar Studios
Microaudio
Royal Exchange Manchester
Sandy Brown Associates
Shure Electronics
Shuttlesound
Sound Technology
Strand Lighting's Tabs Library
Strand Sound
Theatre Projects Services
Turbosound
Vitavox
Yamaha

and especially

John Offord, of Lighting and Sound International
and
Iain Elliott of Canford Audio

INDEX

The following references are not intended to include every mention of each word but to provide the reader with a method of identifying where in the book the main uses of the word occurs, please also see the Glossary on page 130.